I Am:
Excellent & Motivated

Do You Lack Motivation and Feel Stuck at Times?
Weekly Tips that Inspire You to Win!

Mel Frazier-Carroll

Copyright © 2024 by Mel Frazier-Carroll

All rights reserved. No part of this book may be reproduced in any form or by any electronic mechanical means, including information storage and retrieval systems, without permission in writing from the publisher. For permission requests, write to the publisher at the address below.

Salvation Gateway Ministries
14311 Reese Blvd. Suite A2 #397
Huntersville, NC 28078

ISBN 9781733740418

Library of Congress Control Number: 2024915568

All scripture references are taken from the Holy Bible. Specific versions are listed.

Amplified Bible (AMP), Copyright © 2015 by The Lockman Foundation.
Complete Jewish Bible (CJB). Copyright © 1998 by David H. Stern.
Easy-to-Read Version (ERV). Copyright © 2006 by Bible League International.
Good News Translation (GNT). (Today's English Version, Second Edition) © 1992
    American Bible Society.
New International Version (NIV). Copyright © 1973, 1978, 1984, 2011 by Biblica, Inc.
New King James Version (NKJV). Copyright © 1982 by Thomas Nelson.
New Living Translation (NLT). Copyright © 1996, 2004, 2015 by Tyndale House
    Foundation.
The Message (MSG). Copyright © 1993, 2002, 2018 by Eugene H. Peterson.
The Passion Translation (TPT). Copyright © 2017, 2018, 2020 by Passion & Fire
    Ministries, Inc.

Table of Contents

PREFACE **9**
WEEK 1 MOTIVATION **11**
   Motivated to Build 11
WEEK 2 MOTIVATION **14**
   Beware of False Teachers and False Teachings 14
WEEK 3 MOTIVATION **17**
   Beware of Curses 17
WEEK 4 MOTIVATION **20**
   Beware of Curses (part ii) 20
WEEK 5 MOTIVATION **23**
   Facing Reality 23
WEEK 6 MOTIVATION **26**
   Facing Reality (part ii) 26
WEEK 7 MOTIVATION **29**
   Is Anything Too Hard for God? 29
WEEK 8 MOTIVATION **32**
   He's Our Insurance and Assurance 32
WEEK 9 MOTIVATION **35**
   Opportunity 35
WEEK 10 MOTIVATION **38**
   Our Greatest Threat 38
WEEK 11 MOTIVATION **42**
   Navigating the Storm 42
WEEK 12 MOTIVATION **45**
   It's Not Worth It! 45
WEEK 13 MOTIVATION **48**
   Friendship With Who? 48
WEEK 14 MOTIVATION **51**
   Close the Door 51
WEEK 15 MOTIVATION **54**

Get Up and Fight	54
WEEK 16 MOTIVATION	**57**
If It's Not For God, It's Not For Me	57
WEEK 17 MOTIVATION	**60**
It Doesn't Matter!	60
WEEK 18 MOTIVATION	**63**
Just Do It!	63
WEEK 19 MOTIVATION	**66**
Purposeful Pain	66
WEEK 20 MOTIVATION	**69**
Tune Out the Noise	69
WEEK 21 MOTIVATION	**72**
Navigating Inevitable Adversity	72
WEEK 22 MOTIVATION	**75**
Navigating Inevitable Adversity (part ii)	75
WEEK 23 MOTIVATION	**78**
More Than Enough	78
WEEK 24 MOTIVATION	**81**
It's Not Over!	81
WEEK 25 MOTIVATION	**84**
Give it to God	84
WEEK 26 MOTIVATION	**87**
Rest in the Storm	87
WEEK 27 MOTIVATION	**90**
Break the Curse	90
WEEK 28 MOTIVATION	**93**
The Bigger the Attack, the Greater the Shield	93
WEEK 29 MOTIVATION	**96**
Turn to the Previous Chapter	96
WEEK 30 MOTIVATION	**99**
Control What You Can	99
WEEK 31 MOTIVATION	**102**
Don't Limit God	102

WEEK 32 MOTIVATION	**105**
Follow His Lead	105
WEEK 33 MOTIVATION	**108**
God Has the Final Say	108
WEEK 34 MOTIVATION	**110**
Discerning Distractions	110
WEEK 35 MOTIVATION	**113**
Grown Up & Saved	113
WEEK 36 MOTIVATION	**116**
Keep On!	116
WEEK 37 MOTIVATION	**119**
He is For You	119
WEEK 38 MOTIVATION	**122**
Look Back	122
WEEK 39 MOTIVATION	**125**
Not Alone	125
WEEK 40 MOTIVATION	**127**
Patiently Waiting	127
WEEK 41 MOTIVATION	**130**
Trust and Believe	130
WEEK 42 MOTIVATION	**132**
Victory	132
WEEK 43 MOTIVATION	**135**
But God!	135
WEEK 44 MOTIVATION	**138**
But God! (part II)	138
WEEK 45 MOTIVATION	**141**
But God! (part III)	141
WEEK 46 MOTIVATION	**144**
Push	144
WEEK 47 MOTIVATION	**146**
Break Down the Walls	146
WEEK 48 MOTIVATION	**149**

What Do I Do When My Back is Against the Wall? 149

WEEK 49 MOTIVATION **151**
Right is Right, Sin is Sin 151

WEEK 50 MOTIVATION **154**
He is With Us 154

WEEK 51 MOTIVATION **157**
What Will You Do With Your Time? 157

WEEK 52 MOTIVATION **160**
What Happens Next? 160

BONUS WEEK 53 MOTIVATION **163**
Fear of Missing Out (FOMO) 163

BONUS WEEK 54 MOTIVATION **166**
You Only Live Once (YOLO) 166

CONCLUSION **169**
An Important Decision 169

ABOUT THE AUTHOR **171**
Mel Frazier-Carroll 171

Preface

[#motivated]

Have you ever desired to change a behavior or grow in different areas, but different things in your life prevented you from realizing [*getting, fulfilling*] the desire? If you answered "yes", guess what? You're not alone! It's more common than you may think. People fall short on various occasions. This means that people fail to meet expectations or standards at times. What's the reason? Before we answer that question, how about an inspirational quote?

"WE'VE ALL HEARD THE PHRASE 'WE MISS 100% OF THE SHOTS THAT WE DON'T TAKE', BUT WHAT ABOUT WHEN WE MISS 100% OF THE SHOTS THAT WE DO TAKE? DO WE STOP TAKING SHOTS? NOT AT ALL! WE KEEP HOPING THAT WE'LL MAKE THE NEXT ONE."

What did that inspirational quote have to do with our previous question? Absolutely nothing! I just felt like sharing an encouraging quote that sounded wise to make sure that you were being attentive [*insert laughter here*]. Okay, okay, full transparency, I may have used that quote during a half-time speech that I gave to the excellent, excellent, excellent youth basketball team that I coached years ago, but it's still a good one for us to remember. That quote leads to a common message or theme that you'll read in this book, which is excellent motivation. I know you figured that one out because of the title, but act surprised anyway, so that I can continue my half-time speech here. The reason why we often struggle to change, grow, or achieve that goal we dream about is because there's a lack of motivation. This doesn't mean that there's a complete absence of motivation, it means that there's a shortage of motivation that's preventing us from reaching the next level that we desire.

At the beginning of each New Year, I usually ask God for a core theme of the year that will be the focal point of my year. It's no surprise that this year my core theme and focal point is "motivation". It could be a surprise because how would you know? For the purposes of this book, we'll define motivation as, *an individual's desire [want, longing, aspiration] or willingness [eagerness, enthusiasm] to do something*. Motivation must occur prior to goals being fulfilled or challenges being conquered. In other words, we must want to do it and be eager to get it done. If we circle back to the original question about the reasons for changes and growth not being realized in our lives, we can trace the direct link to motivation. The more motivation we have, the more likely we are to realize those goals. The less motivation we have, the less likely we are to realize those goals.

Sounds simple, right? Sounding simple and being simple are two different things. Motivation is not simple at all. It requires something BIG. It requires something GREAT. It requires something that we all need in life. It requires faith, trust, and complete reliance on our Father, God. This is where we get excellence from.

Do you understand the importance of God in our lives? He's the Source for everything essential, everything extra, everything good, and everything excellent. He's our Source for life! Through our faith, hope, belief, and trust in our Lord and Savior Jesus Christ, we're equipped with the tools that we need to be excellent and successful in life. FYI, it's usually best to adopt God's definition of "successful", rather than ours. His definition may not equate to billions of dollars in your account, but an account filled with unlimited peace instead. The point is, whatever we need, the Source can provide. Need motivation? Go to the Source! Need a change in attitude? Go to the Source! Need direction? Go to the Source! No matter the need, go to the Source! If you lack motivation, want more motivation, or want to fill your daily life with motivation, I'm believing that you'll get the appropriate encouragement through this book of spirit-fulfilling weekly devotionals that were written to motivate you to be excellent in every area of your life.

I feel like we're friends already, and because I love you so much already, I'll share my secret with you. Here it is >>> I don't have a superpower, super ability, or super intellect. I simply have the Source in my life, and He provides everything. Everything! In fact, every devotional that you'll read is because of Him. I always ask God to instruct my fingers to type His message that I receive directly from Him. Yes, He speaks to my fingers and my fingers type what's heard directly from Him. His word, not mine. His message, not mine. His praise and glory, not mine. Sounds weird, right? I know, but hey, if we can't be weird [*strange, unusual*] for God our Father and Jesus Christ our Savior, who can we be weird for? Every message that you'll read in this book will be applicable [*appropriate, relevant*] for you, no matter what you're going through in life. Why? Because we all need motivation. Excellent motivation! Therefore, get ready! I mean get really, really, really ready to be #motivated.

Week 1 Motivation

MOTIVATED TO BUILD

∞ ∞ ∞

Hebrews 10:24 [TPT]
Discover creative ways to encourage others and to motivate them toward acts of compassion, doing beautiful works as expressions of love.

Dear Friends,

Another calendar year has begun, which means we've somehow managed to get through all the difficulties that occurred throughout the previous calendar year. Including the calories from the fresh-baked cookies and pies that we chose not to neglect, even though our carb-deprived friends tried to convince us that carbs weren't supposed to come near us. Also, including the many times that we went to the self-checkout line at the store to avoid delays, only to be delayed by the blinking red light that signals "assistance needed". Also, including the many times that we thought we were taking a shortcut only to realize that the new route was even longer than the first route because of road repairs being performed. Yes, we made it past all those challenges and more [*insert laughter here*]. Based on the current times that we're living in some people would consider it a great miracle that we're still able to breathe life and live another year after all the hardships and challenges that were experienced. Let's not take away from the many great things that happened for many people last year, as there were a lot of individuals that experienced an abundance of blessings, joy, peace, and love.

As you can see, different years bring different seasons, different challenges, different blessings, but always the same God. We can always count on God to be faithful in this new year and in future years, just as He was in the previous years. How faithful was He? We're still alive after all the uproar, attacks, battles, and challenges that wrecked many communities across the world. Yes, we're still alive, which should give each of us motivation to build. If all of those weapons formed against you couldn't kill you or destroy you, shouldn't that motivate you? If God's grace was the greatest and most sufficient thing in your life, shouldn't that motivate you? If you're a better you today because of the valuable lessons that you learned yesterday, shouldn't that motivate you? I think so! I think you're motivated right now, even if you don't realize it. So, what will you do with all of the excellent motivation?

> *"THE MORE MOTIVATION WE HAVE FOR GOD, THE MORE LOVE WE HAVE IN OUR LIVES, WHICH HAS ALWAYS BEEN THE CORE MESSAGE OF JESUS CHRIST."*
> *[#motivated]*

Friends, if we wanted to display a lack of gratitude, there are a lot of things in our lives that we could complain about, but there are a lot of reasons to also be thankful. I don't know you, but I'm one-hundred percent sure that there's more good than bad in your life. Completely certain! How do I know? Because there's nothing greater than God and He's in your life. You're still alive because of God, which means His grace, mercy, and perfect love was active in your life, even when you didn't deserve it, and even though you may not have known. With that being said, let's focus on the positive blessings that we have and not the negative circumstances that have occurred. In other words, let's get motivated to build. Build what? Let God help you fill in the blank. Here's a start >>> build on the blessings that you currently have; build on the unlimited love and grace that God has extended to you; build on the irrevocable and forever comforting peace of Jesus Christ that has been made available to you. Keep building because there's so much to be done.

Be motivated to impact the lives of others, as you demonstrate kindness and compassion every day. Be motivated to love unconditionally, just like your Father in heaven loves you unconditionally. Be motivated to be a better you with an even better heart that's complete with joy and a greater level of faith in God. Be motivated to step out of your comfort zone and be the blessing to others that God called you to be. What happens when motivation fills the earth? The earth is filled with accomplishment. Motivation + God = The Passion of Jesus Christ (#love). The more motivation we have for God, the more love we have in our lives, which has always been the core message of Jesus Christ. Love, love, love, and love some more. Be motivated to love! Be motivated to love God, even more. Be motivated to love yourself, even more. Be motivated to love others as you love yourself, even more. This year and every year that follows, let's be motivated to live out the passion of Jesus Christ, which is to love beyond limitation. Are you motivated to build? If so, grab your Bible and let's start building.

DEFINE THE PROBLEM | DEVELOP THE SOLUTION

Think about a time that you chose to keep working or progressing, even though you didn't want to. What were the results of your choice not to give up? At that moment, you were motivated to complete the task and achieve the goal that was set. Remember those experiences and don't forget the will that you possessed. Use that motivation and passion for God. Be motivated to live for Him, completely and wholeheartedly. Don't give up, don't quit, don't take a break! Keep working and progressing. Here's a quick prayer for you, "Father, please help me to remain motivated to live for You. Help me to give You my all. Everything that I am and everything that I have is because of You. You are my everything. My life is incomplete without You. Allow me to be motivated by love every day that I live. In Jesus' Name I pray. Amen."

ENCOURAGEMENT OF THE WEEK [#motivated]

We're all motivated by different things in life, but we're all fueled by the same thing, which is love. Love fuels us and gives us the capacity to live. When we're motivated by love, we're destined to fulfill the will of God.

SPREAD THE MOTIVATION [#motivate]

Encourage someone to be motivated by love. The type of love that goes beyond limitations, restrictions, and barriers. The Type of love that is relentless in representing the Savior Jesus Christ.

Week 2 Motivation

BEWARE OF FALSE TEACHERS AND FALSE TEACHINGS

∞ ∞ ∞

2 Peter 2:1-3 [GNT]

False prophets appeared in the past among the people, and in the same way false teachers will appear among you. They will bring in destructive, untrue doctrines, and will deny the Master who redeemed them, and so they will bring upon themselves sudden destruction. Even so, many will follow their immoral ways; and because of what they do, others will speak evil of the Way of truth. In their greed these false teachers will make a profit out of telling you made-up stories. For a long time now, their Judge has been ready, and their Destroyer has been wide awake!

Dear Friends,

Do you currently have the ability to discern [detect, recognize] a false teaching? A false teaching is anything that goes against, adds to, or takes away from the Word of God. It will often require some type of sacrifice from you or participation in an activity that promises to reward you with knowledge and/or wealth. As noted in the featured scripture, one of the most common motivators of false teachers (and false teachings) is greed. Greed causes bad decisions and terrible transactions. Ecclesiastes 5:10 says, "If you love money, you will never be satisfied; if you long to be rich, you will never get all you want. It is useless" (GNT). Greed is dangerous; it's like an infectious disease that desires to consume and spread. Greed can give birth to greed. In other words, a person that is motivated by greed can detect others that are motivated by greed and is able to cultivate [nurture, promote] their desires of greed.

Have you ever heard of financial seed sowing? If not, it's the backbone of the prosperity teaching in which it is taught (with manipulated scriptural references) that people are able to give money in exchange for things that they hope to receive. It's taught that if you want to receive a house, a luxury car, bigger bank account, successful business, live debt free, or even have better health, sow a seed (make a financial offering) to the church house and you will reap (receive) what you desire. While the concept of giving and generosity is a good, recommended practice, the Word of God doesn't say that we can purchase God's grace, long life, good health, or a successful future. That's a practice of greed exploiting greed. FYI, common manipulated scriptural references are Malachi 3:6-12, Luke 6:38, Acts 2:44-45, and Matthew 10:41. Beware of false teachers and false teachings! Another group of false teachers are those that desire to lead people away from

Jesus Christ, the only Redeemer. Idolatry is their weapon of choice. Idolatry is the worship of something or someone other than God as though it were God, whether intentional or unintentional. You know it's an idol if it's in addition to God or it replaces God.

"IF ANYONE IS ENCOURAGING, PROMOTING, ENDORSING, ADVOCATING, OR SUPPORTING SIN, IT'S A CLEAR INDICATOR THAT SOMETHING IS WRONG."
[#motivated]

Friends, one of the most quoted Bible "sayings" is found in Hosea 4:6, which says, "my people are destroyed for lack of knowledge" (NKJV). While the scriptural statement is true in that a lack of knowledge and awareness will lead to bad occurrences, it's often used in the wrong context. God had this message delivered to the people of Israel long ago because of the heavy influx and practice of idolatry and the worshipping of other gods. It was more about not knowing and acknowledging God (because of idolatry), rather than not having information. Are you aware that continuous sin (iniquity) causes God to be pushed away? Here's something interesting for you to know >>> in Leviticus 18, God told Moses to tell the people of Israel to stay away from the practices of the people of Egypt, where they once lived, and the people in the land of Canaan (modern day Israel), where they were going to live. He specifically gave them forbidden sexual practices. If you were wondering, yes, homosexuality, adultery, incest, and bestiality [*sexual activity between humans and non-human animals*] were mentioned as forbidden practices. Verse 22 says that homosexuality is detestable [*abominable*] to God and verse 23 says that bestiality is perversion, which means God hates it. The interesting part is found in verses 24-29 in which it says that the pagans (those that sinned against God and practiced idolatry) made the land unclean because of all the disgusting things they did, which caused God to punish the land and make it reject the people who lived there. Do you understand that? Those detestable sins (sexual sin and idolatry) caused the land to reject the people.

Do not be deceived. Everything that God warned His people to stay away from was for specific reasons that we often choose to ignore today. Most of the reasons had something to do with covenants and open doors to demonic forces (demons, evil spirits). Beware of false teachers and false teachings! If anyone is encouraging, promoting, endorsing, advocating, or supporting sin, it's a clear indicator that something is wrong. Yes, this includes those that are supportive of sin, especially sin that is known to be detestable to God. Remember, sin is sin. We can like people without supporting sin. Sin caused God to have the land reject the people. The land essentially cried out to God because it was not meant to be filled with sin. FYI, if the land cried out before because of sin, the land will cry out again because of sin. Don't be part of the group that God rejects. The group that chooses not to acknowledge God, rejects Jesus Christ, and embraces idolatry and sexual sin. Friends, if you're currently following false practices, now is the time to turn away. Don't allow greed, sexual practices, or idolatry to lead you further away from God. Don't allow deception and manipulation to influence you into accepting false destructive doctrine and practices. Turn to Jesus Christ, the One that can save you. God doesn't want anyone to be destroyed, but wants all to turn away from their sins (2 Peter 3:9). So, don't wait any longer, repent and be saved. Beware of false teachers and false teachings!

DEFINE THE PROBLEM | DEVELOP THE SOLUTION

Think about a time that you saw others following someone that you knew they shouldn't have been following. Think about some of the warning signs that you saw and apply that logic to your current life. Back then, you had a level of discernment and knew that something was wrong. Now, use the discernment that God freely gives us to recognize false teachers and false teachings, so that you won't be deceived, manipulated, or tricked into following evil masked as light. Here's a quick prayer for you, "Father, please help me to have discernment to recognize false teachers and teachings, and people that have been weaponized by demonic forces to attempt to lead me away from You. Help me to easily recognize, detect, and identify the schemes, tactics, strategies, and tricks that are being used. I commit my life to You and ask that You protect and cover me all the days of my life. In Jesus' Name I pray. Amen."

ENCOURAGEMENT OF THE WEEK [#beware]

Beware of everything that is not truly of God. If it doesn't sound right, test it by measuring it against the Word of God in its true context. False Teachers rely on a lack of knowledge and unawareness, but discernment will expose their intentions.

SPREAD THE MOTIVATION [#motivate]

Encourage someone to not blindly believe or follow others. Let them know about the importance of discernment and awareness.

Week 3 Motivation

BEWARE OF CURSES

∞ ∞ ∞

Proverbs 26:2 [ERV]
Don't worry when someone curses you for no reason. Nothing bad will happen. Such words are like birds that fly past and never stop.

Dear Friends,

Have you ever directed a curse towards someone, or have you ever cursed someone? Many of us may answer with a rapid "no", but that may be because we're not fully aware of what a curse is, so let's look at the definition(s) of a curse. It can be defined as "to call upon divine or supernatural power to send injury upon"; "to bring great evil upon"; "evil or misfortune that comes as if in response to imprecation or as retribution"; "to use profanely insolent language against". No matter which definition we choose to accept, we'll all come to the same conclusion that a curse is not good at all. If we were to completely assess our lives, it's very possible that we would discover that at some point we were involved in a curse, whether as a recipient (curse sent by others towards us) or as a distributor (curse sent to others by us). Curses are brought about through witchcraft, rebellion, and/or ignorance; most are caused by a combination of the three.

Witchcraft involves communication with an evil spirit to gain insight, power, revenge, or a supernatural ability that does not come from God. (Does not come from God!). Common examples include divination, necromancy, magic, sorcery, spells, intuition, levitation, omens, superstitions, fortune-telling, palm-reading, occultism, and things along those lines. Witchcraft will always result in curses. That means one hundred percent of the time, the people that engage in witchcraft will be cursed, whether the participation is intentional or unintentional. Examples of witchcraft and curses that resulted are found throughout the Bible. The Egyptians practiced witchcraft and curses resulted on them (read the book of Exodus); the inhabitants of the land of Canaan practiced witchcraft and curses resulted on them (read Leviticus and Deuteronomy); the Israelites practiced witchcraft and curses resulted on them (read 1 Kings and 2 Kings); the former king of Israel, Saul, lost his life because he consulted with a witch and tried to gain insight from the dead (read 1 Chronicles 10:13-14). Nothing good comes from witchcraft.

Rebellion is disobedience against God. Perhaps the most common types of rebellion are pride and idolatry. 1 Samuel 15:23 notified us that rebellion against God is as bad as witchcraft, and pride is as sinful as idolatry. It's no coincidence that rebellion against God is generally followed by a curse on those that rebelled. (Think about Adam and Eve). Did you know that when we choose to disobey God, we choose to obey Satan and the demon gods/demonic forces? Here's something to always remember >>> pride and idolatry will always cause people to reject God (and Jesus Christ). Always! What happens when we reject Jesus? Jesus said, "Those who reject Me publicly, I will reject before My Father in heaven" (Matthew 10:33, GNT). Is there any curse more significant than getting rejected by Jesus before the Father (Judgment Day)? Nope! If you want to read about all of the major effects of rebellion against God, simply read the Bible, beginning with Adam and Eve (Old Testament). The last form of curses to discuss are curses brought upon by ignorance, which is by far the most common.

"WHEN JESUS DIED ON THE CROSS AND WAS RESURRECTED THREE DAYS LATER, HE DEFEATED EVERYTHING. EVERYTHING! CURSES ARE NO EXCEPTION."
[#motivated]

Friends, one of the greatest weapons used against us is ignorance caused by unawareness. We are all responsible for our own individual unawareness. We cannot blame a pastor, minister, evangelist, teacher, parent, or counselor for our unawareness. The Bible is available to each of us, and it teaches us, guides us, warns us, corrects us, and gives us revelation. Romans 14:10-12 notified us that we will all stand before God to be judged by Him and every one of us will have to give an account to God. That means there are no excuses. Ignorance isn't a valid excuse. Not knowing that you were engaging in idolatry, witchcraft, or rebellion against God isn't a valid excuse. Not knowing about the sinful practices of your ancestors isn't a valid excuse either. Following sinful trends, accepting false teachings, blindly joining groups that practice idolatry, and refusing to accept the unmodified truth (God's Word) are some of the major causes of ignorance. Ignoring the power of our words is another big one. Did you know that many of us communicate curses on a frequent basis? It's sad to hear, but think about it. How many times have you joked about something bad happening to yourself or others? How many times have you spoken a negative label over someone? How many times have you communicated your hopes of something bad happening to someone? These are just some of the common examples of curses that we distribute to others or ourselves. When blessings and curses were spoken in the Bible it was almost a guarantee that they would happen. Why? Because of the power of words. Do you treat your words with careful consideration, or have you been reckless with your words?

It's highly possible that a curse was directed towards you or directed against others by you at some point in your life. So, it's important to break all curses. The only way to do that is through the Curse Destroyer, Jesus Christ. Notice, when Jesus died on the cross and was resurrected three days later, He defeated everything. Everything! Curses are no exception. (See Colossians 2:13-15). We must break the curses by first having Jesus Christ in our lives as our only Lord & Savior. When we say our "only" Lord & Savior that eliminates all options for idolatry. Next, we must repent for every reckless word and deed.

Ask God to reveal to you the curses that have been directed towards you and your bloodline. FYI, we can conclude from reading the Bible that a lot of curses were established by ancestors that either didn't know or didn't care about the effect that their actions would have on their bloodline. Yes, this includes parents, grandparents, great grandparents, and the generations before. The same applies today with the choices that we make. So, cancel, reject, renounce, break, and destroy every curse established against you and your bloodline, and do the same for every curse that you have sent to others. Do it all by the power of the blood of your only Lord and Savior Jesus Christ and do it in His mighty Name. Beware of curses!

DEFINE THE PROBLEM | DEVELOP THE SOLUTION

Can you think of a time that you spoke careless words about yourself or others that resulted in negative things occurring? That's a good example of a curse being spoken and directed towards yourself or others. Our words can be used against us, but they can also be used for good. Allow the Word of God (Jesus Christ) to help you break all of the curses that may have been activated by your words. Here's a quick prayer for you, "Father, please help me to break all curses that I've spoken over myself or others. I submit my life completely to you and I reject, resist, and renounce all agreements, covenants, and partnerships that have been formed with demonic forces. I break and cancel all curses that have been activated by my reckless words. It is through the blood of my Savior Jesus Christ that I have the authority and ability to cancel these curses and agreements, and it is by the blood of Jesus Christ that I cancel all curses. Help me to use my words for good and not for evil. In Jesus' Name I pray. Amen."

ENCOURAGEMENT OF THE WEEK [#aware]

To be aware means to be attentive and alert, and that's exactly what's required of us, so that we don't unintentionally enter into covenants or agreements with demonic forces. Reckless words are an easy entry point for evil. Be aware of the thoughts that you entertain, the actions that you display, and the words that you speak. Submit it all to God and resist all evil.

SPREAD THE MOTIVATION [#motivate]

Encourage someone to break the curses that may have been activated by their reckless words. Let them know that the blood of Jesus Christ can wash away all sins and cancel all curses.

Week 4 Motivation

BEWARE OF CURSES (PART II)

∞ ∞ ∞

Psalm 10:3-4 [GNT]

The wicked are proud of their evil desires; the greedy curse and reject the LORD. The wicked do not care about the LORD; in their pride they think that God doesn't matter.

Dear Friends,

Have you ever participated in a ritual of any sort? It could've been a ritual for religion, fraternity, sorority, gang, family tradition, superstition, social group, political group, or anything. If you have, it's important to be aware that if at any point in the ceremonial or customary activities there was something or someone worshipped or sacrificed to other than the Father (God) and the Son (Jesus Christ), then that qualifies as idolatry. As we learned from the previous messages, idolatry is the worship of something or someone other than God as though it were God, whether intentional or unintentional. Idolatry is detestable to God and forbidden by God (Deuteronomy 4). It doesn't matter if a person is unaware of their participation in idolatry or not, God has strict rules and warnings about idolatry. What's one of the results? A curse. In the previous message, it was noted that curses are brought about through witchcraft, rebellion, and/or ignorance; most are caused by a combination of the three. In other words, curses are the direct result of disobedience. Just like God doesn't tempt people to do wrong (James 1:13-15), God doesn't place curses on people. He allows our actions of obedience or disobedience to determine the outcome of blessings or curses. That means our actions of disobedience place curses on us, not God. That also means God isn't to blame for curses, our actions of disobedience are. Some may ask why do bad things happen to good people, isn't that a curse?

It's important to know that there's a major difference between going through adversity (Challenging times) and being cursed. Adversity is designed to increase our faith and trust in God during and after experiencing challenging times. The lives of Joseph (Genesis 37-41) and Daniel (Daniel 1-6) are examples of that. Jesus already warned His followers that we'll face adversity in life (John 16:33) and we won't be accepted by the world because of our relationship with Him (John 15:18-21). Remember, the world represents everything that goes against God (sin, evil, wickedness, darkness, etc.). If the world won't accept us because of Jesus, then the world will try to convince us to be like them. How? By attempting to get us to tolerate sin, accept sin, and participate in sin. The featured scripture notified us that the wicked are proud of their evil desires, curse and reject the LORD, do not care about the LORD, and think that He doesn't matter. The world succeeds when a follower of Jesus Christ engages in any act of disobedience.

> *"WHEN JESUS DIED ON THE CROSS AND WAS RESURRECTED THREE DAYS LATER, HE DEFEATED EVERYTHING. EVERYTHING! CURSES ARE NO EXCEPTION."*
> *[#motivated]*

Friends, there are countless scriptures in the Bible that warns us not to participate in the sinful activities practiced by those that have chosen to reject God. Be extremely cautious before blindly following trends, traditions, false teachers & teachings, and knowingly or unknowingly practicing idolatry. 1 Corinthians 10:20-21 notified us that, "What is sacrificed on pagan altars is offered to demons, not to God. And I do not want you to be partners with demons. You cannot drink from the LORD'S cup and also from the cup of demons; you cannot eat at the LORD's table and also at the table of demons" (GNT). What's the result of such behavior? Let's go back to the beginning where the advanced warnings were provided. "Cursed is anyone who carves or casts an idol and secretly sets it up. These idols, the work of craftsmen, are detestable to the LORD'" (Deuteronomy 27:15, NLT). Let's look at another one in Deuteronomy 12:30-32, which says, "After the LORD destroys those nations, make sure that you don't follow their religious practices, because that would be fatal. Don't try to find out how they worship their gods, so that you can worship in the same way. Do not worship the LORD your God in the way they worship their gods, for in the worship of their gods they do all the disgusting things that the LORD hates. They even sacrifice their children in the fires on their altars. Do everything that I have commanded you; do not add anything to it or take anything from it" (GNT). Yes, you read that correctly, they sacrificed their physical children in the literal fire on their altars to attempt to please their demon gods. Today, when people practice idolatry, they may not be sacrificing their children physically, but they are spiritually. They're offering up their children, involving them in their covenants, and giving their demon gods the legal right to be a part of their children's life.

There are many, many more warnings throughout the Bible, Old Testament and New Testament. The point is, there is no need to add additional philosophies to God's Word, nor is there a need to add suspicious practices or created things in your worship of God. Such behavior isn't motivated by God, encouraged by God, or led by God. It is deception designed to lead God's people astray and into a curse that spreads through generations because of a covenant that gets formed with demonic forces/demon gods. Don't fall for the trap and the same strategy that has been used since the beginning of time by Satan and his demonic forces, which is to cause us to question, doubt, and challenge God's Word. We know the Truth, so allow the Truth to set you free. Who's the Truth? Jesus Christ! What's the Truth? The Gospel of Jesus Christ, the Word of God! Jesus Christ is the Curse Destroyer, Life Giver, Redeemer, Savior, and the Bridge of Reconciliation that reconciles us to the Father. Repent for your sins, the sins of your parents, grandparents, and ancestors that may have established covenants with demonic forces/demon gods through acts of disobedience and let Jesus Christ break the curses. The blood of Jesus Christ purifies us, sanctifies us, and washes us clean. We are made new in Christ Jesus. He is the Way, the Truth, and the Life (John 14:6). Let Him be the only Lord and Savior of your life. God doesn't want any of us to be cursed or perish because of disobedience. He wants each of us with Him. Let's make a choice to choose Jesus Christ and live for God. Beware of disobedience and beware of curses.

DEFINE THE PROBLEM | DEVELOP THE SOLUTION

Think about a time that you knew the right thing to do, but you chose not to do it. That's an example of disobedience. Disobedience opens the door to negative consequences and curses. Curses don't just affect you, but can also be passed down to children and continue through bloodlines (generations). Don't allow disobedience to be a factor in your life. Choose obedience to God. Learn from the warnings, previous mistakes, and resulting consequences, and avoid disobedience at all costs. Whatever the temptation is, know that it's not worth it. Here's a quick prayer for you, "Father, please help me to deny the desires of my flesh that attract me to sin. Help me to not give in to uncontrolled emotions and uncontrolled thoughts, but allow me to submit everything to You. I choose to submit my flesh, my thoughts, my desires, and everything that I have to You. Help me to resist all temptation and reject all lust and evil. Help me to be pure in heart with motives of love. I choose You over myself. In Jesus' Name I pray. Amen."

ENCOURAGEMENT OF THE WEEK [#choose]

God gives each of us the ability to choose what type of life we want to live. It can be a life of blessings through obedience to Him, or it can be a life of curses through disobedience to Him. God is extremely fair because He allows our actions to determine the result. Choose life! Choose God! Choose obedience to Him!

SPREAD THE MOTIVATION [#motivate]

Encourage someone to fully consider the ramifications of the temptation to sin against God by doing what He said not to do. Disobedience will lead to curses that could and should be avoided.

Week 5 Motivation
FACING REALITY

∞ ∞ ∞

2 Timothy 3:1-5 [AMP]

But understand this, that in the last days dangerous times [of great stress and trouble] will come [difficult days that will be hard to bear]. For people will be lovers of self [narcissistic, self-focused], lovers of money [impelled by greed], boastful, arrogant, revilers, disobedient to parents, ungrateful, unholy and profane, [and they will be] unloving [devoid of natural human affection, calloused and inhumane], irreconcilable, malicious gossips, devoid of self-control [intemperate, immoral], brutal, haters of good, traitors, reckless, conceited, lovers of [sensual] pleasure rather than lovers of God, holding to a form of [outward] godliness (religion), although they have denied its power [for their conduct nullifies their claim of faith]. Avoid such people and keep far away from them.

Dear Friends,

Have you ever wondered why things in life happen the way that they do? If you answered 'yes', you're not the only one. I used to wonder why my hairline didn't remain impermeable [resistant, unaffected] to age (it's okay to laugh, I won't be offended) [*insert laughter here*]. A lot of things can't be explained, but there are some unfortunate things that can be explained through the Bible. In fact, the Bible gives us all a heads up about many of the things that we'll see in our lives. In the featured scripture, we read about some unfortunate and difficult truths of what is referred to as the last days. Keep in mind, the last days is an extended period that began after the physical earthly departure of Jesus Christ. Because no one except God knows when Jesus Christ will return, any day moving forward can become the last day, which is why we're living in the last days. In these last days, there will be a lot of wickedness.

If we were to observe the world around us, we'll notice a very harsh reality that Jesus Christ is not loved or liked by a lot of people today. Yes, the same Jesus Christ that died for our sins, so that we could have life and be reconciled to the Father. It's unfortunate, but true. Many people are choosing themselves over Jesus, as they place their love for themselves and the fulfillment of their lustful desires and pleasure over everything and everyone in their life. Many people are choosing their love of money, wealth, and power over Jesus, as they're motivated and impelled [driven, encouraged] by greed to build prosperity by any means necessary, possess as much resources as possible to feel fulfilled, and obtain as much power, authority, fame, and popularity as they could possibly get. FYI, those are all examples of idolatry. For many individuals, Jesus is simply an afterthought or fictional character in a book with a bunch of made-up stories and contradicting rules for hypocritical [phony, two-faced] religious people. Sounds fairly accurate, right? I think each of us can think of a handful of people that we've come across that share some of these beliefs and views, correct? Again, we were forewarned about the wickedness, evil, craving of sin, and everything else that goes against God. Some may even say that our current society is among the most godless and selfish society in history. While we may not be able to confirm or deny that opinion, we can observe some of the things that were mentioned about the last days. So, what do we do?

"THERE'S NO BENEFIT FOR GAINING THE WORLD WHILE LOSING YOUR SOUL AND FORFEITING YOUR LIFE IN THE PROCESS."
[#motivated]

Friends, let's consider Matthew 7:13-14 in which Jesus says, "Go in through the narrow gate; for the gate that leads to destruction is wide and the road broad, and many travel it; but it is a narrow gate and a hard road that leads to life, and only a few find it" (CJB). Here's a shocking truth that you may not have known >>> following Jesus Christ is not the popular choice. Many people may say that following Jesus requires too much sacrifice of happiness, too much restriction of pleasure, too many unnecessary rules, and no fun at all because of the need to have self-control and self-discipline. It's a narrow gate and a hard road, not because there's more life difficulty and more hardships, it's because it's not the norm. It's not popular, which means it goes against what others are usually doing. Wouldn't it be easier and more enticing [desirable, attractive] to simply join the crowd and follow the broad road and wide gate? But, at what cost? There's no benefit for gaining the world while losing your soul and forfeiting your life in the process (Mark 8:36). There's no benefit for living life with a void in your heart that you'll never be able to fulfill on your own. The void is a big, big, big emptiness that can only be fulfilled by Jesus Christ. It can't be fulfilled by a husband or wife, it can't be fulfilled by children, it can't be fulfilled by money, it can be fulfilled by fame, it can't be fulfilled by pleasures, possessions, or achievements, it can only be fulfilled by Jesus Christ and the immeasurable love that comes from Him.

It's true that we must face the harsh reality that Jesus is not the popular choice in the world that we live in, but we can't be afraid to choose the unpopular hard road and narrow gate. This is the choice that will guarantee us life. If we choose Jesus, we have full assurance that we'll never be alone. He'll be with us all the days of our lives, which means we'll always be able to overcome whatever is sent our way to challenge us because of His sufficient grace. Let's make the right choice and choose Jesus Christ. Jesus Christ is our reality.

DEFINE THE PROBLEM | DEVELOP THE SOLUTION

Think about the decisions that you often make, both major and minor, and determine if Jesus is a part of those decisions on a continuous basis. If we're constantly making decisions without our Lord and Savior Jesus Christ, we're constantly missing out on His wise counsel and sufficient blessings, so invite Him to be with you each day as you make decisions. Here's a quick prayer for you, "Father, please help me to live in full unity with You through Jesus. Allow me to always choose Jesus over the world and all of its influences. My life is Yours. All that I have and all that I am is Yours. I humbly submit and surrender completely to You. In Jesus' Name I pray. Amen."

ENCOURAGEMENT OF THE WEEK [#sacrifice]

Sacrifice is essential in any healthy relationship. Sacrifice enables selflessness and paves the way for unity. Our relationship with God through the Savior Jesus Christ requires sacrifice; it requires us to give Him our everything, so that He can have full oversight of our lives. Allow God to be your Source for everything in your life.

SPREAD THE MOTIVATION [#motivate]

Encourage someone to choose Jesus and represent Him by demonstrating love, peace, joy, kindness, compassion, and being relatable.

Week 6 Motivation

FACING REALITY (PART II)

∞ ∞ ∞

James 4:4-6 [AMP]

You adulteresses [disloyal sinners—flirting with the world and breaking your vow to God]! Do you not know that being the world's friend [that is, loving the things of the world] is being God's enemy? So, whoever chooses to be a friend of the world makes himself an enemy of God. Or do you think that the Scripture says to no purpose that the [human] spirit which He has made to dwell in us lusts with envy? But He gives us more and more grace [through the power of the Holy Spirit to defy sin and live an obedient life that reflects both our faith and our gratitude for our salvation].

Dear Friends,

Have you ever experienced a situation in which you were caught in the middle of two people or two groups that wouldn't get along? No matter what was said or done, you knew for certain that it was impossible for both sides to reconcile. I can relate, as this happens to me when I visit the bakery and instantly get pulled in the middle of the battle for my taste buds between fresh-baked cookies and fresh-out-of-the-oven pies [*insert laughter here*]. Fortunately for us, whether knowingly or unknowingly, we face this reality every day of our lives. Yes, you read that correctly, the word "fortunately" was used and not "unfortunately" (keep reading, you'll understand why). If you're able to remember the message, "Facing Reality", then you'll know that there's some type of choice that must be made daily. FYI, if you don't remember the message, turn to the previous message. The featured scripture gives us a glimpse of the choice that must be made, as it says, "Whoever chooses to be a friend of the world makes himself an enemy of God". When we choose to love the things of the world (sinful desires), we make our choice to go against God. Let's put this in the proper context.

On one side, there's the world and all of its appealing attractions, including everything that would be desirable for the flesh (sinful nature). Just in case you're wondering what this could include, think about money, power and control, fame, influence, social media followers, lustful relationships (sexual), wealth, possessions, glory, worship and praise, recognition, acceptance from everyone, and the list goes on and on. Get the point? Although very pleasurable and attractive, choosing the world's side can be extremely costly (remember Mark 8:36?). On the other side, there's God - the Creator, Savior, and Deliverer. This side is highlighted by an overwhelming, immeasurable, sufficient amount of love and grace. It's the exact opposite of the world. It doesn't look as attractive, doesn't seem as exciting, and it doesn't seem to offer the luxurious pleasures and self-fulfilling achievements or advancements. It doesn't promise or guarantee unlimited riches, fame, followers, or lustful relationships. It doesn't give you the ability to be worshipped or idolized for the things that you're able to do. This side has standards, rules, principles, morals, and values to live according to. This side promises eternal life with God, which is something that the other side takes away. So, you're currently stuck in the middle and you must decide which side is best for you. Remaining neutral is not an option and both sides will never get along. It's impossible for a compromise or sacrifice. It's either all or nothing with your choice. Both sides want you to choose one side, so which side do you choose?

"THROUGH THE POWER OF THE HOLY SPIRIT, HE GIVES US THE ABILITY TO DEFY SIN AND LIVE AN OBEDIENT LIFE THAT REFLECTS OUR FAITH IN HIM AND OUR GRATITUDE FOR SALVATION."
[#motivated]

Friends, before you choose a side today, consider this response that Jesus gave the people, as noted in Matthew 12:30, "Anyone who is not for Me is really against Me; anyone who does not help Me gather is really scattering" (GNT). That message speaks for itself; commentary [explanation, clarification] is not necessary. We are faced with a difficult decision each day. A decision in which we can either choose God or the world. It sounds simple when we read it in a text, but when reality confronts us and demands that we make an immediate choice on the spot, the choice becomes much more difficult than it seems. Need an example? Consider the Apostle Peter who was a disciple and student of Jesus that often fellowshipped with Jesus for a few years and undoubtedly loved Him, but denied Jesus when faced with the tough reality of having to choose his safety or potential persecution. As you may be aware, he chose his safety and denied knowing Jesus because he feared the potential harm that could've happened to him if he admitted to being one of Jesus' disciples. Need more examples? Let's consider all of the times that emotions guided actions. The times when lust was allowed to override love and destroy relationships. The times when anger was allowed to override peace and cause havoc and chaos. The times when greed was allowed to override gratitude and lead to treacherous [unfaithful, deceitful] decisions. The times when sin was allowed to override self-control and lead to self-destruction. Can you identify with any of those examples?

Many of us are guilty of choosing the world over God at some point in our lives. But God! God gives us grace and mercy. Through the power of the Holy Spirit, He gives us the ability to defy sin and live an obedient life that reflects our faith in Him and our gratitude for salvation. God equips us with everything that we need to make what was once a difficult choice become an easy choice. Friendship with the world or friendship with God? That's the choice that needs to be made. Are you going to choose God or the world? This is the reality that we face every day. A choice must be made each day by everyone. A choice that has fruitful benefits (blessings) as well as severe consequences (curses). There's only one choice to make. There's only one choice that guarantees eternal life with God, and that choice is Jesus Christ. Choosing Jesus Christ (choosing God's side) unites us with God and gives us the fulfilling life that we need, on earth and after earth is gone. We're not promised or guaranteed the attractive things of the world, but we are guaranteed victory through Christ. Jesus Christ is our reality.

DEFINE THE PROBLEM | DEVELOP THE SOLUTION

Think about the temptations that you face on a consistent basis. Be fully aware of the causes of temptation and the potential weaknesses that you have. Temptation occurs when there's a desire, want, or interest in something that should be avoided at all costs. God helps us stay guarded against temptation through the power and discipline of self-control, so don't battle temptation without Him. Here's a quick prayer for you, "Father, please help me to not give into temptation or sinful desires that surround me. Help me to stay rooted in You and in Your values and principles that You have provided me. Allow me not to be controlled by my fleshly desires, but be led by Your Spirit, as I humbly submit and surrender completely to You. Lead me and guide me as only You can. In Jesus' Name I pray. Amen."

ENCOURAGEMENT OF THE WEEK [#discipline]

Discipline is a key part of self-control. It allows restraint and considers the impact, effect, or resulting consequence of a particular action. The more we submit to God, the more we're able to overcome temptation through the fruitful power of self-control.

SPREAD THE MOTIVATION [#motivate]

Encourage someone to not give into temptation and make bad decisions that could and should be avoided. Let them know that God gives us the ability to see the trap and resist the bait, always.

Week 7 Motivation

Is Anything Too Hard for God?

∞ ∞ ∞

Matthew 19:26 [GNT]
Jesus looked straight at them and answered, "This is impossible for human beings, but for God everything is possible."

Dear Friends,

Is anything too hard for God? This is a rhetorical question, meaning an answer is not expected because the answer is already known. The answer is no! Nothing is too hard for God! However, our actions don't always reflect that true statement. Have you ever been in a very difficult situation that usually results in negative consequences [bad outcomes], but somehow, someway it didn't end that way for you? Have you ever made it through a period of challenges and difficult times [hardship, adversity]? It's no surprise, coincidence, or shock that we made it through those situations and difficult times. It wasn't by luck or happenstance [chance]. It wasn't the universe, science, deceased ancestors, idols, or the gods of the world that helped you get through it. It was God! God made it possible because all things are possible with God. This includes the things that we think are impossible, according to our limited worldview.

It's fair to state that our view of God must change if we are guilty of placing limitations on His ability. Although it's difficult to not do, we must not base God's abilities on our limited human logic and reasoning. We can't reduce God to our limited human standards. We'll never be able to comprehend God. Have you ever had toys or dolls that you played with when you were younger? If so, were any of those toys or dolls ever able to understand how you thought, how you reasoned, how you chose to love, or even how you used your wisdom and creativity to interact with them? Of course not! That's just a mini portrayal [representation] of our ability to understand God. He's the Creator and we're the created. He knows everything, sees everything, hears everything, and is in full control of everything. Without the knowledge that He gives us, we know nothing. He's God and we're His creation.

"IF WE ALLOW GOD TO BE OUR GOD, HE WILL BE OUR GOD. IF WE ALLOW OTHER GODS TO BE OUR GOD, GOD IS FORCED TO HONOR OUR CHOICE."
[#motivated]

Friends, let's go back to the initial question and add to it. Is anything too hard for God (in your life)? What big problems are you facing? What unfortunate situations are confronting you? What strongholds seem too great to overcome in your life? What goals and aspirations seem unlikely or unrealistic in your life? Whatever your answers are, stop and give it to God! Stop! Give it to God! I know, I know, you've heard it all before, it's the same thing once again, but have you really tried to give it to God, completely [totally, entirely]? I don't mean tried it for a few days or a few weeks. Have you really tried giving everything to God? That requires complete faith, hope, belief, and trust in Him. Do you know that a young man was thrown into a lions' pit to be slaughtered by ferocious lions (yes, multiple lions), but was completely protected by God and unharmed by the lions? That young man was Daniel (read Daniel 6). Do you know that three young men were thrown in a fiery furnace to be burned to death, but were completely protected by God and unharmed by the fire? Those three young men were Hananiah (Shadrach), Mishael (Meshach), and Azariah (Abednego) (read Daniel 3). Do you know that a Savior was crucified on a cross and died, but three days later was resurrected by God and defeated death? You already know that Savior's Name, it's the Name that is above all names, the Name of Jesus Christ. The same God that did all of those impossible and miraculous things is the same God that you and I serve and is the same God that continues to have oversight [supervision] of our lives, if we allow Him to.

If we allow God to be our God, He will be our God. If we allow other gods to be our god, God is forced to honor our choice, which means He allows us to reap the destruction that the other gods bring. It's important to know that God has given complete authority to His Son Jesus Christ (Matthew 28:18), and has made Jesus the gateway [entry, access] to Him (John 14:6). No Jesus Christ equals no God. With Jesus comes victory, faith, hope, assurance, joy, strength, and a level of peace that cannot be measured. Through Jesus, we're able to give all of our problems and difficulties to God. Through Jesus, we're able to remain calm and can rejoice during any type of adversity. The love of God is immeasurable [great], incomprehensible [can't be understood], unimaginable [unbelievable], and uncontainable [can't be controlled]. It's greater than anything that exists in our lives. His love for us is the very reason why nothing is too hard for God. Live your life full of faith in Him and know that nothing is too hard for God.

DEFINE THE PROBLEM | DEVELOP THE SOLUTION

Think about a time that you faced a big challenge and had little to no faith, but God intervened and rescued you despite your little to no faith. Did you learn from that experience? Whether you did or didn't, now is the time to remember how bad it could've been if it wasn't for God helping you out. He's our refuge and shelter always. It's important for us to not place ourselves in harmful situations, but continue to submit to God and obey His directions for us. Here's a quick prayer for you, "Father, please help me to remove all of the limitations that I place on You. Help me to never doubt Your ability to do the impossible. What's impossible for us is possible for You. Help me to not place myself in harmful situations caused by my disobedience to You, but instead help me to obey You and trust that You will never lead me into temptation or into the hands of evil. I trust You completely. In Jesus' Name I pray. Amen."

ENCOURAGEMENT OF THE WEEK [#limitless]

God is without limits or limitation, which means His ability is limitless. His love is limitless, His grace is limitless, the peace He gives us is limitless. Don't place limitations on God, trust Him to do the impossible and provide the miraculous solution that only He can provide.

SPREAD THE MOTIVATION [#motivate]

Encourage someone to know that God can do anything. It doesn't matter how big, difficult, unusual, or unlikely the situation is, God can do the impossible.

Week 8 Motivation

HE'S OUR INSURANCE AND ASSURANCE

∞ ∞ ∞

Hebrews 9:15 [NLT]

That is why He is the One who mediates a new covenant between God and people, so that all who are called can receive the eternal inheritance God has promised them. For Christ died to set them free from the penalty of the sins they had committed under that first covenant.

Dear Friends,

Are you familiar with the terms 'Insurance' and 'Assurance'? Although the two terms sound very similar, they're slightly different. Insurance can be defined as a type of coverage via a contract in which one party agrees to indemnify [cover, protect, reimburse] the other party for loss that occurs under the terms of the agreed upon contract. In other simpler words, it's an agreement of protection and coverage. Assurance can be defined as full confidence and certainty; promise or pledge; and freedom from doubt. So, if we think about the two terms, one essentially lets us know that we're covered by a contract, and the other lets us know that we can have full confidence in the promise or pledge. Can you think of a time that you had assurance in your insurance (Auto insurance? Home insurance? Health insurance?)? Hopefully, the insurance contract didn't have any fine print limitations. What are fine print limitations? The very important terms and conditions that are generally missed because they're written in the smallest font and are in the most ignored section possible. Although an insurance contract gives us some protection and some confidence of coverage, can we be fully certain that it will be enough to sustain [support, maintain] us? Maybe not. Isn't there Someone that can give us full confidence of coverage? Absolutely! That Someone is our Father God.

God has established a covenant with each of us, which is like a promise, agreement, and/or contract. His covenant is full of sufficient protection and coverage that are equivalent to promises without any fine print limitations. Unlike standard insurance agreements, this covenant isn't limited to an underwriter [sponsor, backer] that evaluates our potential risk to determine the amount of coverage that should be offered to us. Our covenant has a Mediator that intercedes for us and guarantees us unlimited coverage, despite our liability, risk, shortcomings, flaws, blemishes, and imperfections. That Mediator is Jesus Christ, the Messiah. Jesus isn't concerned about the risks of insuring us.

In fact, He prefers to cover the riskiest individuals, including the broken, the sick, the lost, the hurting, the neglected, the abused, the addicted, the vulnerable, and the list of imperfect people goes on and on. Our Mediator's coverage of grace extends beyond our ability to fathom [understand, comprehend], and it's sufficient for each of us.

> *"IF WE ALLOW JESUS TO BE THE CENTER OF OUR LIVES, WE WILL ALWAYS BE FULLY COVERED AND PROTECTED THROUGHOUT THE COURSE OF OUR LIVES."*
> *[#motivated]*

Friends, Jesus Christ is our Insurance and Assurance in this life that we live. We can put our full trust in Him and confidently stand on the terms of His covenant. Consider some of these terms: (1) whoever believes in Jesus shall not perish but have eternal life (John 3:16); (2) no one can see the kingdom of God unless they are born again (John 3:3); (3) no one can get to the Father except through Jesus (John 14:6); (4) seek first His kingdom and His righteousness, and all your needs will be provided (Matthew 6:33); and (5) nothing will be impossible for you if your faith is in Jesus (Matthew 17:20). The terms are simple. If we allow Jesus to be the center of our lives, we will always be fully covered and protected throughout the course of our lives. In addition to the coverage, we'll be beneficiaries [recipients, receivers] of His perfect love and unlimited grace, which leads to blessings that we won't be able to count.

It's extremely important that we allow Jesus to be what He's supposed to be in our lives, and that is our Lord, Savior, Redeemer, and Everything. It doesn't matter what trials we're going through; the coverage terms will always remain intact. He has overcome the world and has equipped you and I to do the same. Nothing can break us, and nothing can forcefully take away our faith, prayer, peace, and joy. Sure, we may get knocked down and may even experience loss during different periods in life, but let's be reminded that everyone that chooses to put their complete trust in Him will never be put to shame (Romans 10:11). Let's be reminded that every trial we experience in life will produce perseverance and endurance, which will build our character, and increase the level of hope and assurance that we have in our Messiah (Romans 5:3-4). Let's be reminded that we have been given victory through our Lord Jesus Christ (1 Corinthians 15:57). We can and will overcome all things through Jesus Christ. Our insurance policy is fully guaranteed assurance. It was signed and sealed with the blood of our Mediator, Jesus Christ. Therefore, let's live our lives with freedom from doubt and with full certainty knowing that our God is always with us, and we are always covered by Him.

DEFINE THE PROBLEM | DEVELOP THE SOLUTION

Think about all the times that you suffered loss and what you thought was defeat. Now, think about all the times that you bounced back and were able to somehow get more than what you lost and have victory. It's no coincidence that you survived and thrived. It's all because of God's love, grace, and intervention in your life. Keep trusting, depending, and relying on Him to be your Source for life. Here's a quick prayer for you, "Father, please help me to always remember that You're in full control. Although the problems and challenges may seem too difficult to overcome, I can and will trust You to be everything that I need to continue living life completely submitted, committed, and surrendered to You. I am certain that I have victory through my Lord and Savior Jesus Christ. In Jesus' Name I pray. Amen."

ENCOURAGEMENT OF THE WEEK [#protection]

We all need and want security in our lives. It's essential to our growth and survival in a variety of areas. God's protection is the exact security that we need. His protection not only keeps us from harm, but it also delivers us from evil, equips us with full armor, and gives us wisdom to remain under His covering.

SPREAD THE MOTIVATION [#motivate]

Encourage someone to remember that we can have full confidence and assurance in God because He's in full control. Nothing can happen in any of our lives without His consent.

Week 9 Motivation

OPPORTUNITY

∞ ∞ ∞

1 Corinthians 10:13 [TPT]
We all experience times of testing, which is normal for every human being. But God will be faithful to you. He will screen and filter the severity, nature, and timing of every test or trial you face, so that you can bear it. And each test is an opportunity to trust Him more, for along with every trial God has provided for you a way of escape that will bring you out of it victoriously.

Dear Friends,

What do you think of when you hear the word "opportunity"? Do you ever associate it with challenges and adversity? I don't think many people would consider adversity as an opportunity because we often consider opportunities as good things that bring us happiness and cause us to feel good, but that's not the case with adversity, right? Do you ever feel good about adversity? I'm talking about the type of adversity that attempts to break you, test your faith, and demand your patience. Need an example? Imagine going to a gas station that has no gas, while your gas tank is empty. For all of my electric vehicle friends, imagine going to a charging station that has no charge, no electric boost, or no power, while your battery is extremely low. Get the point? Those are situations that many of us would avoid if we could, but sometimes we can't.

Here's the good news >>> adversity is only as bad as our outlook [attitude, mindset] and perception [view, opinion] of the circumstance. In the featured scripture, we're reminded that each of us will go through times of testing because it's a normal experience in life. Although we'll go through some type of adverse circumstance that makes us want to give up or wallow [stumble, stagger, revolve] in our emotions, we're also granted the opportunity to trust God even more. God screens and filters the level of difficulty, the extent of danger, and the length and duration of the test or trial, so that we can bear it, endure to the end, and eventually persevere through Him. He gives us the opportunity to trust Him and follow His way of victory.

"We need God every second of every minute of every hour of each day. He's the Power Source that gives us light. He's the Compass that leads us to where we must go in life."
[#motivated]

Friends, although things may be difficult right now, consider those challenges, struggles, problems, tests, trials, and tough times that you're facing or have faced as opportunities to elevate your trust in God. Consider them as opportunities to conquer and overcome through God. God is faithful. He doesn't abandon us in good times, and He'll never abandon His children in adverse times. His love is unconditional. The question that we should all ask ourselves is, "am I faithful to God?". Are you? Do your tests and trials draw you closer to God or push you further away from Him? Does your prosperity [wealth, success] draw you closer to God or push you further away from Him? FYI, nothing should ever get in the way of us being fully united with our Father God and our Lord and Savior Jesus Christ. If something or someone is causing you to neglect your relationship with God, it's time to reevaluate and reassess that idolatry-filled situation and get back on track. Nothing is worth being away from God.

Can you imagine driving a car on a road without any stop lights, stop signs, or street signs? Can you imagine walking around your neighborhood without any light and being in complete darkness? Hard to imagine, right? That's what living life without God is like. It's not worth it! We need God every second of every minute of every hour of each day. He's the Power Source that gives us light. He's the Compass that leads us to where we're supposed to go. So, the next time that you're facing some type of adversity, after you take some time to process the situation (remember, we're human beings and sometimes it takes us a few minutes/hours to fully process our thoughts and emotions in a healthy manner), consider it an opportunity to trust God even more. Consider it an opportunity to rely on the strength that the Lord and Savior Jesus Christ provides us through His comforting Spirit. Don't focus on the problem or the test, focus on the opportunity. Victory awaits you!

DEFINE THE PROBLEM | DEVELOP THE SOLUTION

Think about a time that you faced a test or trial that you were not expecting. Consider all of the negative emotions that you felt and compare those to the actual opportunities to learn and grow that resulted from the experience. Allow those experiences to help you remember that there's an opportunity on the other side of the problem. Here's a quick prayer for you, "Father, please help me to approach all problems and tests with the appropriate mindset, self-control, outlook, and perspective that You give me to understand that there's an opportunity to learn, to grow, to overcome, and persevere. Help me to focus on You and the victory that You provide. In Jesus' Name I pray. Amen."

ENCOURAGEMENT OF THE WEEK [#opportunity]

Opportunities and faith go together. When challenges, problems, tests, and trials confront us, we must look past the negatives and focus on the positive, which is our belief that an opportunity to succeed and excel will be established. There's always an opportunity to grow in Christ.

SPREAD THE MOTIVATION [#motivate]

Encourage someone to know that there's generally a positive found in each negative situation, if we change our outlook and perspective, and allow God to be our complete Source.

Week 10 Motivation

OUR GREATEST THREAT

∞ ∞ ∞

1 Kings 19:1-5 [NIV]

Now Ahab told Jezebel everything Elijah had done and how he had killed all the prophets with the sword. So, Jezebel sent a messenger to Elijah to say, "May the gods deal with me, be it ever so severely, if by this time tomorrow I do not make your life like that of one of them." Elijah was afraid and ran for his life. When he came to Beersheba in Judah, he left his servant there, while he himself went a day's journey into the wilderness. He came to a broom bush, sat down under it and prayed that he might die. "I have had enough, LORD," he said. "Take my life; I am no better than my ancestors." Then he lay down under the bush and fell asleep.

Dear Friends,

When you think about a threat, what's the first thing that you think of? Some people may think about danger, others may think about risk, others may think about the devil and his demonic forces, and others may think about that old rival they had that competed with them for best in the class, best in the department, best on the team, or best in the social circle. Yes, it's true, we've all had some type of rival in our days that was considered a potential threat to what we wanted to accomplish. It's also true that of all the things I mentioned thus far, none of them are our greatest threat in life. I know this may be very surprising, but the devil and his demonic forces aren't our greatest threat in life. Don't get me wrong, they are a major threat, definitely top three, but there's something even greater. Let's look at the featured scripture for clues.

In the featured scripture, Elijah had just been threatened by the wicked Jezebel who was Ahab's wife. Ahab was the king of Israel at the time, and he married Jezebel, daughter of Ethbaal, king of the Sidonians. FYI, it may not be a good idea to name your child Jezebel. If you want to know why Jezebel's father was mentioned, it's because of her bloodline. The Sidonians originated from Canaan. That's the same Canaan that fathered the Canaanites. Those are the same Canaanites that worshipped demon gods and sinned against God, causing the land to reject them, which allowed the Israelites to take over the land. The Israelites were warned against making treaties or alliances with the Canaanites and other inhabitants of the land, and were told to not marry any of them, and not allow their children to marry any of them because they would lead them away from God to worship other gods. Ahab was the king of Israel that ruled in Samaria and chose to marry a Canaanite woman. So, what do you think happened? 1 Kings 16 says that Ahab was guilty of doing a lot of wicked things that aroused the anger of the LORD more than all the kings of Israel before him. He not only married Jezebel, but he also built a temple to Baal (demon god), made an altar for him and put it in the temple, and put up an image of the goddess Asherah (another demon god). The simple translation for all of that is, he openly rebelled against God and disobeyed God, which brought curses on himself and the land. Fun Fact: Ahab's father was former king of Israel, King Omri, who sinned against the LORD more than any of his predecessors, and he's the person that built the town of Samaria after purchasing the land from a man named Shemer (1 Kings 16).

Now that the introduction of the main characters is complete, let's proceed with the story. It starts with Elijah delivering news to Ahab that there would be a great drought in the land as he said, "As the LORD, the God of Israel, lives, whom I serve, there will be neither dew nor rain in the next few years except at my word" (1 Kings 17:1, NIV). The LORD then told him to leave and hide in a certain location where he would drink from the brook and be supplied with food by ravens. Yes, you heard that correctly! The LORD had ravens supply Elijah with food. A few years later, the LORD told Elijah to go and present himself to Ahab and He would send rain on the land. There was a major problem though. Ahab had been searching for Elijah for a very long time and Jezebel had been killing off the LORD's prophets. During the first interaction between Ahab and Elijah, after years had passed, this is what Ahab said to Elijah, "Is that you, you troubler of Israel?" (1 Kings 17:17, NIV). After a few exchanges, Elijah told Ahab to summon the people from all over Israel to meet him on Mount Carmel and bring the four hundred and fifty prophets of Baal and the four hundred Prophets of Asherah (all of them were wicked to God).

As the people arrived, Elijah prepared to lay down the ultimate challenge, the epic battle of the ages. In order for the people to determine whose God was real, Elijah challenged the prophets of Baal to a battle in which both sides would get two bulls, cut them into pieces and put them on the wood, but not set fire to it. The people would know whose god was real by the one that answered by fire. The prophets of Baal went first and called on the name of Baal from morning until noon, but no answer. They shouted, they danced around the altar, and they continued their frantic prophesying, but still no response. It was now Elijah's turn. He had the altar repaired with twelve stones that represented the tribes that descended from Jacob. He had the people fill four large jars with water and they poured it on the offering and the wood. After He prayed to God, fire of the LORD fell and burned up the sacrifice, and the people fell prostrate and cried, "The LORD—He is God! The LORD—He is God!" (1 Kings 18:39, NIV). It didn't stop there. Elijah commanded the people to seize the prophets of Baal, and he had them slaughtered. Then he told Ahab that rain was coming. So, he had the wicked "prophets" (those that practiced witchcraft) slaughtered and then mentioned that rain was coming (the curse of drought would end).

This leads us to the featured scripture in which Jezebel heard what happened and sent a death threat to Elijah. Because Jezebel was a woman with a lot of power and influence, Elijah was afraid and ran for his life. It didn't stop there. Elijah prayed for God to end his life, but of course that's not how the story ended. God did not end Elijah's life, and He allowed Elijah to gain a successor as prophet in the prophet Elisha.

"THERE WILL BE MANY WEAPONS FORMED AGAINST US THROUGHOUT THE COURSE OF OUR LIVES, BUT NONE WILL PROSPER IF WE'RE EQUIPPED WITH GOD'S ARMOR."
[#motivated]

Friends, now that we're aware of the story, can you identify what our greatest threat in life is? No, it's not our enemies. No, it's not our closest friends or loved ones that know a lot of concealed things about us and can potentially cause a lot of harm through betrayal. Okay, I'll tell you. It's our emotions. Yes, we are the greatest threat to ourselves. Think about it. Elijah was the prophet of God that witnessed many events take place at the hands of God. He witnessed a long drought, a miracle of daily bread, and a dead boy returning to life (1 Kings 17). He also witnessed fire coming down from heaven, ravens feeding him mornings and evenings, and rain returning after the great drought. He witnessed all of those things and more, but because he was afraid, he may have forgotten what God could do. He believed that his fate would be like that of the other prophets like him (prophets of the LORD); the ones that were killed at the order of Jezebel. He believed that he was all alone, the only one left. That's what our uncontrolled emotions will do. It'll convince us to accept mistruth as fact. Elijah gave into fear and allowed that fear to take away his peace.

How many times have we allowed our uncontrolled emotions to take away our peace, our faith, and even our right-standing with God? Do you remember the popular verse of Isaiah 54:17 that says, no weapon formed against you shall prosper? That message was declared long ago and it's still applicable [appropriate, relevant, valid] today for each of us. Uncontrolled emotions are a threat that causes us to harm ourselves and those around us. The uncontrolled emotions also cause harm to those that are supposed to be recipients of blessings that come from our faith and obedience to God. Uncontrolled emotions will cause us to exchange God's promises for Satan's lies. Don't give into fear. Don't give in to anxiety. Don't allow worry and distress to make decisions for you. If we control our emotions, our emotions won't control us. The greatest "emotion-controller" is self-control, which is freely given to us because of our relationship with Jesus Christ. Yes, self-control is a very important fruit and gift produced by the Holy Spirit (Galatians 5:23). Therefore, limit your greatest threat's ability to harm you by trusting God, no matter what's happening around you. Always have self-control.

DEFINE THE PROBLEM | DEVELOP THE SOLUTION

Think about a time that you wanted to run and hide because of fear. What happened? Did the thing or person you feared end your life? Obviously not because you're reading or listening to this message right now. The point is, trust God! Nothing happens without God's consent. Nothing! He has committed to protecting us and providing for us as a Father does for His children. Keep trusting Him! Here's a quick prayer for you, "Father, please help me to keep trusting You at all times. Help me to never take my eyes off You and help me to never take my hope off Your Word. Your Word is a promise to me and my brothers and sisters, so let us hold it near and dear to our hearts. Let us live completely for You. In Jesus' Name I pray. Amen."

ENCOURAGEMENT OF THE WEEK [#restraint]

Life requires us to have restraint. Restraint must be at hand when dealing with emotions. Restraint must be at hand when confronting challenges. Restraint must be at hand when submitting to God. We need restraint, which allows us to not surrender to our will, but surrender to God's will and plan for our lives.

SPREAD THE MOTIVATION [motivate]

Encourage someone to maintain self-control, even amid heightened emotions. Not many good decisions are made when uncontrolled emotions are at hand.

Week 11 Motivation

NAVIGATING THE STORM

∞ ∞ ∞

Mark 4:37-41 [CJB]

A furious windstorm arose, and the waves broke over the boat, so that it was close to being swamped. But He was in the stern on a cushion, asleep. They woke Him and said to Him, "Rabbi, doesn't it matter to You that we're about to be killed?" He awoke, rebuked the wind and said to the waves, "Quiet! Be still!" The wind subsided, and there was a dead calm. He said to them, "Why are you afraid? Have you no trust even now?" But they were terrified and asked each other, "Who can this be, that even the wind and the waves obey Him?"

Dear Friends,

Have you ever experienced a bad storm that challenged your faith as well as your safety and level of preparedness [being fully prepared]? This is what the disciples experienced in the featured scripture. A storm so bad that they feared for their lives. They must have realized that they weren't prepared for a storm of this magnitude. Try to understand what they were going through and imagine that you're on the boat with them. What would you do? Running is probably the first thought, but there's nowhere to run, is there? Let's pause here for a quick true story.

"Once upon a time there lived a very cool individual that we'll call Mel. One day, as Mel was washing his vehicle in his driveway, he noticed a wild animal resembling a baby black bear headed in his direction. He wanted to make sure that the children in the neighborhood were safe, so he made up his mind to try to get the attention of the bear and maybe ask it very nicely, very, very politely, to leave the area (maybe not a good idea, right?). As the animal moved closer, Mel realized that it wasn't a bear, it was just a very large dog on the loose. So, this very cool and brave individual, named Mel, got the attention of the dog and asked it to leave, maybe not as politely as he would've asked the bear, but still somewhat politely. Well, the dog didn't respond as friendly as Mel would've hoped, and the large dog began to run towards him very aggressively, very quickly, and very angrily while barking with its war cry that probably resembled the war cry that caused the wall of Jericho to fall. Mel considered his options in this potential storm and decided that running was his preferred choice of action, unfortunately for Mel there was a small problem (maybe "small" isn't the best word to use), he was suddenly unable to run. His mind and brain said run, but his feet didn't get the message that was being relayed from his brain.

He couldn't run. Yep, nowhere to run, just like the disciples on the boat. If you're wondering what happened, Mel was unharmed because of...yes, you guessed it correctly, the intervention of his Father God and his Savior Jesus Christ. How lovely and safe it is to be covered by God and the Savior Jesus Christ [insert laughter here]".

Now, let's get back to the message. If you were with the disciples on the boat, would you have focused your attention on the storm or would you have focused on your trust in Jesus? Believe it or not, many people have experienced similar non-physical storms of great magnitude [size, extent]. The doctor reports that put an estimated expiration on a person's life, the fertility results that gave unexpected news, the termination of employment from a company of many years, the heartbreak of betrayal, and the list goes on and on. The potential for destruction accompanies each storm, but let's pay close attention to the actions of the disciples. Despite fearing for their lives, they chose to go to Jesus. What should we do?

"WE SERVE A SUPERNATURAL GOD THAT EQUIPS HIS SONS AND DAUGHTERS WITH SUPERNATURAL STRENGTH CALLED FAITH."
[#motivated]

Friends, our response to adversity is just as impactful as the adversity that we face. In other words, how we respond to the storm is equally important as the storm that confronts us. Storms can only destroy us if we allow them to. We can lessen the impact by being prepared. How can we prepare for a storm? Start with faith. There's a reason why we've made it this far in life, and it has nothing to do with luck or chance or the universe. It's because of God's grace. His unlimited and sufficient grace. God has extended grace upon grace to His children, to those He call His sons and daughters. His grace has sustained us through the symbolic hurricanes that sought to destroy us; the tornados that tried to disrupt our relationships; and the typhoons that attempted to devastate everything in and around us. His grace has been and will continue to be sufficient for each of us, no matter what the storm is. So, how will you choose to navigate the storm?

How about we resist the urge to give in to fear and choose to stand firm in faith? From a natural perspective, fear is an easier choice than faith. It's easier to believe what we can see, instead of trusting in what we cannot see, but we serve a supernatural God that equips His sons and daughters with supernatural strength called faith. Faith in Jesus Christ can move mountains, calm storms, and conquer fear completely. Therefore, let us not operate with a natural perspective, but a faith perspective. Let's remind those storms that our God is greater. We may be in the eleventh hour and the storm may seem as if it's going to prevail and destroy us, but our God is undefeated, and He will always be victorious. Victory has already been guaranteed to us through Jesus Christ our Savior. We will persevere and overcome through our faith in Him. So, let's remember this as we navigate the storms in life through our complete faith in Jesus Christ.

DEFINE THE PROBLEM | DEVELOP THE SOLUTION

Think about a situation that you did not want to be in, but somehow, someway you ended up in, by no fault of your own. The situation could have gone a lot worse than it did, but you chose to remain calm and remembered what you were taught previously from the Word of God. The Word of God kept you from harm, equipped you with faith and calmness, and prepared you for the experience, so remember to allow faith in God and trust in His Word to help you remain calm during any storm. Here's a quick prayer for you, "Father, please help me to always choose Jesus Christ. Whether I'm in a storm or experiencing harvest, please allow me to always remember Your Word and the instructions that You provide me. Help me to always be willing, able, and prepared to always represent Jesus Christ. In Jesus' Name I pray. Amen."

ENCOURAGEMENT OF THE WEEK [#prepared]

Being prepared requires thoughtful consideration and foundational knowledge. There is no greater foundation than God's Word, emphasized by the life and love of Jesus Christ. The more we live according to Jesus, the more prepared we are for any challenge that is sent our way.

SPREAD THE MOTIVATION [#motivate]

Encourage someone to plan not to fail by accepting the plans of God, which starts with complete faith and trust in Jesus Christ. When we make God's plans our plans, we live according to His purpose and protection.

Week 12 Motivation

IT'S NOT WORTH IT!

∞ ∞ ∞

Proverbs 25:28 [MSG]
A person without self-control is like a house with its doors and windows knocked out.

Dear Friends,

Have you ever done something wrong that you regretted later? Think beyond that bad haircut, it'll grow back. Think beyond those desserts that you couldn't say "no" to last week; you'll end the relationship with those overly friendly calories soon [*insert laughter here*]. If the answer to the initial question is "yes", what was your reason for doing the regrettable action? In most cases, we make bad choices when we allow our uncontrolled emotions to lead us. In other words, it happens when we lack self-control, which usually occurs during a period of vulnerability, disappointment, or anger. When an expectation is not met, different emotions generally occur. Intense anger is probably the most common result. When individuals are filled with intense anger or rage and they act on those emotions, they're usually unable to consider the negative consequences that will most likely occur afterwards. Their only focus is on that point in time. This is a very common example of an uncontrolled emotion. Keep in mind, anger is a natural emotion for human beings. We'll all experience anger at some point in our lives. However, as noted in Ephesians 4:26, anger must not be uncontrolled, it must not lead us to sin, and it must not be held onto for extended periods. Otherwise, we give a foothold or open invitation to the devil and his demonic forces to reside with us. No one should ever want that. Anger is just one example of the different emotions that we experience.

This message isn't limited to anger, it includes all emotions that are often uncontrolled and result in regret. Consider the featured scripture, which says, "a person without self-control is like a house with its doors and windows knocked out". Think about a house without windows and doors. How safe would you feel in that house? You wouldn't be able to rest peacefully in those unsafe conditions because there would always be a potential threat. The same situation applies for individuals that lack self-control and allow their emotions to remain uncontrolled. There's always the threat of a bad decision or action that they will regret afterwards, which usually affects those around them as well. If only there was an alarm that could go off in our head and give us a signal when we're about to make a big mistake that we'll regret later.

"EVERY ACTION THAT OFFERS YOU A POINT IN TIME PLEASURE OR SATISFACTION AT THE EXPENSE OF YOUR LONG-TERM PEACE IS NOT WORTH IT."
[#motivated]

Friends, we do have an alarm that alerts us and even helps us avoid those actions that we'll regret later. That alarm is the Holy Spirit. As a result of the active presence of Jesus Christ in our lives, the Holy Spirit is with us always, providing us non-stop counseling, guidance, discernment, insight, and foresight. Through the Holy Spirit, we're able to know when something is simply not worth it. Self-control is a direct gift from the Holy Spirit, which means if you have Jesus in your life, you also have the ability to maintain self-control, which also means before you make those mistakes that you will most certainly regret later, you are able to think about everything carefully and be instantly reminded that, "It's not worth it!". Those four words are very important in life. They keep us from crossing lines, help us remain within moral boundaries, and most importantly, keep us from giving in to temptation. Put it into action moving forward.

The next time you're tempted by that something or someone, think about the damage that could occur to your household, yourself, and your relationship with God, and the shame and regret that will most likely occur and say, "It's not worth it!". The next time you're filled with raging anger because of an offense or disappointment, think about the long-term impact and the regret that will most likely occur and say, "It's not worth it!". It's not worth it! Revenge is not worth it! Rebellion is not worth it! Pride is not worth it! Greed is not worth it! Hatred and unforgiveness is not worth it! Lust is not worth it! Every action that offers you a point-in-time pleasure or satisfaction at the expense of your long-term peace is not worth it. It's a trick and a trap intended to deceive you into thinking that that's the best choice for you. Don't give in to your uncontrolled emotions. Don't turn a mute ear to the Holy Spirit. Don't make the mistake that will cause you to be filled with shame, regret, and a lack of peace. You're stronger than temptation. You're wiser than the deception. You're covered by God. Remember that when these peace-stealing situations occur and attempt to lure you into the trap, and remind yourself that, "It's not worth it!".

DEFINE THE PROBLEM | DEVELOP THE SOLUTION

Think about a time that you faced temptation and wanted to give in, but just when you were about to make that mistake that you would've regretted, something prevented you. That something wasn't a coincidence, it was God sending you a reminder that the point-in-time pleasure was not worth the negative consequences that would've resulted. Don't neglect or ignore the Holy Spirit's warnings and the discernment that is given to you. Nothing is worth sacrificing your relationship with God. Here's a quick prayer for you, "Father, please help me to always maintain self-control. Keep me from all harm, danger, and temptation. Help me to submit completely to the Holy Spirit's counsel and guidance and not allow my flesh to lead me. I choose You! In Jesus' Name I pray. Amen."

Encouragement of the Week [#self-control]

To not be led by uncontrolled emotions, we must have self-control. Self-control keeps us from giving in to temptation, prevents us from self-destruction, and helps us control our emotions. Submit to God and maintain self-control each day of your life.

Spread the Motivation [#motivate]

Encourage someone to maintain self-control, which will prevent them from making mistakes that they will regret later. Help them to remember that "It's not worth it!".

Week 13 Motivation

FRIENDSHIP WITH WHO?

∞ ∞ ∞

James 4:4-7 [GNT]

Unfaithful people! Don't you know that to be the world's friend means to be God's enemy? If you want to be the world's friend, you make yourself God's enemy. Don't think that there is no truth in the scripture that says, "The spirit that God placed in us is filled with fierce desires." But the grace that God gives is even stronger. As the scripture says, "God resists the proud, but gives grace to the humble." So then, submit yourselves to God. Resist the Devil, and he will run away from you.

Dear Friends,

How many times have you been in unfortunate circumstances? Of those times, how many were because of your own doing? In other words, how many times have you placed yourself in unfortunate circumstances because of the decisions and choices that you made? One of the biggest choices in life is choosing the company that we keep. Who or what we surround ourselves with is important for our growth and development in life. I may or may not have previously surrounded myself with an excess of fresh-baked goods (cookies, pies, and cakes), fried fish, and soft serve ice cream disguised as frozen yogurt, instead of the treadmill, bicycle, and jump rope. Don't judge me, I'm getting back on track [*insert laughter here*]. In the featured scripture, James addressed a very important subject of bad friendship. Before we discuss it in greater detail, let's look at a helpful and relevant proverb that says, "Don't be envious of evil people, and don't try to make friends with them" (Proverbs 24:1, GNT). Bad friendships can be very detrimental [harmful, damaging]. If you had a choice between a rich, powerful, and popular friend that often did wrong things or an average, conservative, unpopular friend that lived for God, which one would you choose? Be honest!

Think about your answer, which will help you examine your heart. Let's look at the guidance from James, as it says, "Don't you know that to be the world's friend means to be God's enemy? If you want to be the world's friend, you make yourself God's enemy" (James 4:4, GNT). This doesn't mean cancel all of your friendships with people that aren't walking the same walk as you, unless God is leading you to do that because it's better to be obedient to God than submissive to your flesh. The guidance provided by James means that we must fully examine ourselves and determine what's truly in our heart. If we're craving the world, which represents the sinful nature and the deceptive attractions of sin, then that's an indicator that we desire friendship with the world. That's equivalent to wanting friendship with the devil, demonic forces, darkness, evil, and everything that comes along with it. Something that's missing from the friendship with the world fine print is that more will be taken from you then is given to you. Lust, money, success, and the rest of the attractions may be given to you, but it will cost a lot. Your life, soul, fate, and bloodline effects are just some of the victims that will be caught in the crossfire and transactions. In the end, that friendship will place you in unfortunate circumstances. What's the solution?

> *"WHEN WE CHOOSE TO SUBMIT TO GOD, WE HUMBLE OURSELVES BEFORE HIM AND REBALANCE OUR PRIORITIES IN LIFE TO MAKE THEM ALL ALIGN TO HIS WILL."*
> *[#motivated]*

Friends, if we continue to read the guidance it says, "Submit yourselves to God. Resist the devil and he will run away from you" (James 4:7, GNT). That's the solution in a nutshell. Fun fact: "nutshell" is an idiom [phrase, saying, expression] used to replace the phrase "in as few words as possible". Submitting to God is the answer today, tomorrow, the next day, and every day that follows. When we choose to submit to God, we humble ourselves before Him and rebalance our priorities in life to make them all align to His will. The priorities will shift from self and selfish desires to God and His desires (His will and purpose) for our lives. Would you rather be friends with God or the devil? Sounds like a silly question, right? However, it's a question that many of us answer unknowingly through the choices that we make in life. Choosing the world and chasing after sin is the same as choosing to be friends with the devil. If you're wondering, it's impossible to be friends with both. It's one or the other. God, the Creator of life or the devil, the ruler of evil.

How do you discontinue a bad habit? Yes, this is a real question for you. What's your answer? Discipline, self-control, replacement, etc. may work temporarily, but without God that bad habit can resurface at any time. At any period of vulnerability, any period of weakness, any period of discouragement or loneliness. This is why it's extremely important to submit to God. God has never hidden the fine print from us, instead He has made known the end from the beginning. Friendship should be based on trust, love, and reliability amongst many others. Does that sound like friendship with the world? Can you trust the devil to be a loving and reliable friend? Of course not! But God! God is everything our soul desires. God is love and He fills us with His perfect love. In fact, we were made perfect in His love. Does that mean we are without flaws? Nope! The birth of sin ensured we'd be exposed to it at some point in life on earth, but we can choose God. We can choose to humble ourselves, submit to God, and resist the devil and all evil. We can have evil flee from our lives. Yes, we can resist and reject all evil. It starts with us willingly choosing to be friends with God and the Savior Jesus Christ. Friendship with who? With the One that saves!

DEFINE THE PROBLEM | DEVELOP THE SOLUTION

Think about what you want in life. Think about what you hope to gain, accomplish, and do while you have life on earth. Now think about where God fits in those plans. If He's not at the very top of the list, at the center of everything, and the focus of all plans, that's an indicator that something needs to change. Don't choose anything or anyone over God. Prioritize Him, always. Here's a quick prayer for you, "Father, please help me to rebalance my life's priorities to ensure that You're always the priority in my life. Let all of my decisions and choices be motivated by glorifying You wholly and truly. Help me to cherish my friendship with You. I love you with all of my heart, mind, and soul. In Jesus' Name I pray. Amen."

ENCOURAGEMENT OF THE WEEK [#resist]

To resist the devil, all evil, and sin, we must humble ourselves and submit to God. This means we must deny ourselves and allow God to be the Lord over our lives. For this reason, we have Jesus Christ ready and available to be the Lord and Savior of our lives. All we have to do is let Him in.

SPREAD THE MOTIVATION [#motivate]

Encourage someone to examine their heart to see if they desire God or the world. Let them know that there's no comparison between the two. God cannot be matched and His love for us will always be too great to measure.

Week 14 Motivation

CLOSE THE DOOR

∞ ∞ ∞

Genesis 4:7 [NIV]
"If you do what is right, will you not be accepted? But if you do not do what is right, sin is crouching at your door; it desires to have you, but you must rule over it."

Dear Friends,

    Have you ever answered the door without checking to see who was there? Just in case you're tempted to blame the lack of a peephole or eyehole in your door or the absence of a smart camera for your actions, there's always an upstairs window that you could've used to communicate with your visitor, even though the entire neighborhood would've probably heard the conversation. This approach is considered highly effective in some cultures (I grew up in Brooklyn, NY and am speaking from first-hand experience, as there were people yelling from windows daily) [*insert laughter here*]. Back to the point. You probably answered the door because you were unbothered by the unknown [unspecified, undetermined, unidentified]. Did you know that we often do the same thing spiritually? Yes, it's true. Our actions are equivalent [equal, comparable, same as] to us opening the door. For example (FYI, I enjoy examples), when we choose to tell lies, we open the door for deception and manipulation. When we choose to gossip, we open the door for judgment of others, jealousy, and monitoring spirits (demonic spirits that monitor behavior, actions, tendencies, conversations, etc.). Do you understand the point? Our actions are prerequisites [requirements, conditions] to the things that we experience in life. It's important for all of us to know that there's a physical world (things that we can naturally see) and a spiritual world (things that we cannot see with our natural eyes). You may have heard terms like "supernatural", "unconscious", "universe", "atmosphere", "realm", or "kingdom", right? These are all terms used to describe the spiritual world. So, yes, the spiritual world does exist. God exists, His angelic beings exist, and the fallen angelic beings (devil and his demonic forces) exist.

    Now that we are aware of that, let's focus on the featured scripture in which God tells Cain that if he does not do what is right, sin is crouching at his door. Remember, our actions determine whether we open the door for sin. If Cain is disobedient to God and does the wrong thing, the door will be opened for sin. Keep in mind, when the door is opened for sin, bad things happen. Sin never travels alone; it brings heavy baggage with it. What may start out as just a simple harmless lie, can easily lead to stealing, cheating, and killing, why? Because sin doesn't travel alone. This is why God told Cain that sin desires to have him, but he must rule over it. The same guidance applies to us today. FYI, if you're not familiar with Cain, he ended up killing his brother Abel because of jealousy.

> *"OUR ACTIONS ARE PREREQUISITES [REQUIREMENTS, CONDITIONS] TO THE THINGS THAT WE EXPERIENCE IN LIFE."*
> *[#motivated]*

Friends, there's nothing new under the sun. That's a nice biblical line that may or may not be easily understood. The full scripture comes from Ecclesiastes 1:9, which says, "What has been will be again, what has been done will be done again; there is nothing new under the sun" (NIV). It means exactly what it says, what has been done before will be done again in some form. So, yes, before there was an iPhone, there was a revolutionary Motorola Dynatac 8000X cellular phone (nicknamed "the brick") that may have been the size of a large tablet or small laptop and weighed over a pound, but it was still revolutionary. Revolutionary! [*insert laughter here*]. Why is this important to remember? Because we can learn from the lessons of old. The warning and guidance that God gave Cain long ago is still applicable today for each of us. Sin desires to separate us from God. The more we sin, the further we move away from God.

Imagine a sign on the front door of your neighbor's house that says, "The door is unlocked, enter whenever you want". Think about the danger that could occur. A lot of vandalism [damage], theft, harm, and destruction. That's the same thing that happens to us when we choose to open the door for sin. An invitation to sin paves the way for the devil and his demonic forces to enter in and cause vandalism, theft, harm, and destruction in a person's life. The result is undetected strongholds, generational curses, and loss of life. None of us should desire that. God didn't create us to be willingly oppressed by demonic forces. God created us to be free from sin and to remain united with Him. Good news, John 8:36 says, "If the Son sets you free, you will be free indeed", which means sin has no power over you if Jesus Christ has set you free. What's the prerequisite? Acceptance and continued obedience to Jesus. It may sound simpler or more difficult than it is. The point is that an active relationship with Jesus is equivalent to having a sufficient [satisfactory, appropriate] door guard. No threats are allowed to enter.

Is the door to your heart guarded or unguarded? If you're living without a sufficient door guard (Jesus Christ), it's time for you to make a change. Remember, the spiritual world exists and we're at the forefront of the unseen battle that's occurring. So, it's important for us to choose a side. Good or evil? Do not open the door for sin, nor the devil, nor evil, nor the demonic forces, nor the strongholds that desire to lead you to self-destruction. Sin is wandering around the world seeking souls to devour. If our actions go against God, an invitation for sin is sent out. Don't open the door to sin. Close the door on sin by submitting and committing to God. Submit to God, resist evil, and it'll flee. Sin cannot and should not remain at your front door, make it go away by choosing Jesus. No more delays, choose Jesus Christ!

DEFINE THE PROBLEM | DEVELOP THE SOLUTION

Think about a time that you opened the door to things that you knew were bad for you and the negative impact that it had on your life. A lot of harm could've occurred, but there were lessons learned. Learn from those experiences and mistakes and let that motivate you to never open the door to sin again. Here's a quick prayer for you, "Father, please help me to avoid opening the door to sin. Help me to know, understand, and discern when something is not for me. Help me to always choose You and never allow sin to be my companion in life. I submit and commit my complete life to You. In Jesus' Name I pray. Amen."

ENCOURAGEMENT OF THE WEEK [#freed]

It's important to remember that sin has no power over us if we don't give it power. If Jesus Christ is our Lord and Savior, and we remain obedient to Him, He has given us the ability and authority to rule over sin because of His victory over sin. It's an inheritance of victory that we are given because of His love for us. So, remember that Jesus has freed you from the power of sin.

SPREAD THE MOTIVATION [#motivate]

Encourage someone to know that they are no longer prisoners of sin that are stuck in bondage because Jesus Christ has delivered and freed them completely.

Week 15 Motivation
GET UP AND FIGHT

∞ ∞ ∞

Galatians 5:16-17 [NLT]
So, I say, let the Holy Spirit guide your lives. Then you won't be doing what your sinful nature craves. The sinful nature wants to do evil, which is just the opposite of what the Spirit wants. And the Spirit gives us desires that are the opposite of what the sinful nature desires. These two forces are constantly fighting each other, so you are not free to carry out your good intentions.

Ephesians 6:10-12 [NLT]
A final word: Be strong in the LORD and in His mighty power. Put on all of God's armor so that you will be able to stand firm against all strategies of the devil. For we are not fighting against flesh-and-blood enemies, but against evil rulers and authorities of the unseen world, against mighty powers in this dark world, and against evil spirits in the heavenly places.

Dear Friends,

If you were asked to describe an enemy, what would your response be? Wait! Your in-laws (the ones that criticize your cooking and nearly everything else that you do) or those grade school rivals aren't the type of enemies that we'll focus on. Although it seems like an easy question, it's challenging to answer. If we look closely, we'll see that the featured scriptures already provide us with the answer (hint-hint: it's bigger than opponents, competitors, rivals, and people that dislike us). With everything that's occurring in the world today, it's very easy to become distracted and lose focus of what our life mission is and who our true enemy is.

Before proceeding, let's revisit the attention-grabbing title of the message, which is "Get Up and Fight". "Fight" is a triggering word, so let's not immediately shift our thoughts to physical combat, boxing gloves, or mixed martial arts; it's not that type of fight we're talking about here. Focusing on the physical aspect would cause us to limit the battle to the surface level, while neglecting the true mastermind that's hidden from our view. The true fight isn't against other human beings, it's against the evil forces in the world that are unseen – the devil, demonic forces, and the flesh (sinful nature). Chaos, division, fear, pride, rebellion, worry, doubt, constant quarreling and fighting, and disobedience to God are all descriptors of an environment that the devil is well-pleased with. If these descriptors describe your life, your household, or your community, then the devil is well-pleased with the disorder that is present. Remember, the devil is in complete opposition [disagreement, conflict] with God. If the devil is well-pleased with the disorder, that means God is not pleased at all. The problem occurs when we stop focusing on God and start focusing on everything else. When God is removed from the scenario or when God is no longer the focus of the scenario, the scenario will become vulnerable to the manipulation [influence, control] of the devil. Don't just believe it because I said it, test it out for yourself. Think about everything that's bad in your life or around you and see if God has been the focus the entire time. If we're completely honest with ourselves, we'll arrive at the same conclusion. When God is not the focus, sin infiltrates [intrudes, interferes] the situation and wreaks havoc over time. What do we do now?

"PRAYER ASSEMBLES AN ARMY OF FAITH, HOPE, BELIEF, TRUST, SELF-CONTROL, PEACE, AND JOY THAT UNITES US WITH GOD'S WORD AND SUSTAINS US."
[#motivated]

Friends, we must get up and fight! How do we fight? We pray! Prayer assembles an army of faith, hope, belief, trust, self-control, peace, and joy that unites us with God's Word and sustains us. Therefore, get up and fight! We get up and fight against the urge to accept fear, doubt, and worry, and we do not give those peace-stealers access to lead and govern our thoughts and actions. We get up and fight against the urge to allow pride, rebellion, depression, sadness, grief, and rage to reside in our minds and in our households. We get up and fight against the strongholds that have been allowed to remain in our lives for far too long because of generational factors (bloodline curses), self-constructed hazards (bad decisions), or attacks against our lives (warfare). We get up and fight against everything that is not of God, everything that is not for God, and everything that is against God. We get up and fight against the evil rulers and authorities of the unseen world, against the mighty powers in this dark world, against the evil spirits in the heavenly places, and against the sinful nature. We get up and fight! We don't fight against our black neighbors, our white neighbors, our brown neighbors, or any other color neighbors, or human beings that are different than us. We fight against the sin and demonic forces that infiltrate our environments and seek to cause chaos, destruction, and division. That's what we fight against.

Keep in mind, if we attempt to fight alone, we'll lose every time. We have a Big Brother in Jesus Christ that we can run to for help. We have a Big Brother in Jesus Christ that has already defeated the "baddest" of the bad, the strongest of the strong, and the toughest of the tough. We have a Big Brother in Jesus Christ that has told each of us, including the weary and burdened, to come to Him and He will give us rest. We have a Big Brother in Jesus Christ that has told us in advance that we will have trouble in this world, but take heart (don't let it bother you) because He has overcome the world. Jesus has overcome the world and every sin that attempts to destroy us and wreak havoc in our lives. What do we do now? We armor up with the full armor of God and we get up and fight. The victory is already ours through Jesus Christ.

DEFINE THE PROBLEM | DEVELOP THE SOLUTION

Think about a time that you were in an intense battle with sin. Every time you tried to move on, sin attempted to pull you back into a bad habit, a bad environment, or an addiction. You tried and tried to do it on your own, but it didn't work. It didn't work because Big Brother Jesus Christ wasn't called upon to help you. Learn from those past mistakes and invite Jesus to always join you, especially in the battles that you face. Victory is inevitable when Jesus Christ is in the mix. Here's a quick prayer for you, "Father, please help me to never attempt to fight a battle on my own. My Lord and Savior Jesus Christ has already won the battle. Help me to remember that and trust You to grant me victory through Jesus. No matter the opposition, let me trust You to be all that I need. In Jesus' Name I pray. Amen."

ENCOURAGEMENT OF THE WEEK [#prayer]

Prayer is one of our greatest tools for battle. It's a weapon that will never be insufficient, it'll never require maintenance, and it'll always be available to us for every battle. Prayer is the answer! Use prayer to aid you in the fight against sin, you'll win every time because Big Brother Jesus Christ will be with you.

SPREAD THE MOTIVATION [#motivate]

Encourage someone to keep praying, believing, trusting, and having faith while going through the battles and opposition that they're experiencing. God will never abandon His faithful children.

Week 16 Motivation

IF IT'S NOT FOR GOD, IT'S NOT FOR ME

∞ ∞ ∞

1 John 3:7-10 [NIV]

Dear children, do not let anyone lead you astray. The one who does what is right is righteous, just as He is righteous. The one who does what is sinful is of the devil, because the devil has been sinning from the beginning. The reason the Son of God appeared was to destroy the devil's work. No one who is born of God will continue to sin, because God's seed remains in them; they cannot go on sinning, because they have been born of God. This is how we know who the children of God are and who the children of the devil are: Anyone who does not do what is right is not God's child, nor is anyone who does not love their brother and sister.

Dear Friends,

    If you had to assess [evaluate, measure] your daily life, would you say that your life is filled with "wrong"? In other words, do you often do what is considered "wrong"? Many people will quickly respond with a "no", not because it's factual, but because of the worldly standards that are being measured against. Are you aware that morals, values, principles, and standards constantly change in the world that we live in today? Today, sin is celebrated and even encouraged at times, causing many people to forget what sin truly is. Some people may limit sin to the extremely evil, wicked acts of cruelty such as unprovoked murder, terrorism, acts of violence, major theft, sexual crimes, and distribution of harmful drugs, but is that accurate? Is sin limited to those acts? Is there a full list of sins for us to reference, other than the ten commandments? Some would argue that we define what truth is ourselves and our inner being will alert us of what's right and what's wrong (I believe the term used is "moral compass"). Some would argue that we can't simply rely on the Bible because there are a bunch of contradictory [conflicting, differing] scriptures that will confuse us, since the Bible is "man-made". Others would argue that the laws of the country that we live in will determine what's right and what's wrong.

    Keep in mind, if we're the deciding factor of what's right and wrong, the standards will continue to change because they'll be based on our conditions, emotions, and circumstances. The world will be the world, and God will be God. God is the single Source for what's right and what's wrong. We don't have to find an answer or search for a missing answer because God is the answer. God is righteous, God is good, God is right, and God is the Decider of righteousness and sin. If you believe that the Bible is contradictory, know that it isn't. The New Testament is composed of writings that highlight key occurrences of the life of Jesus Christ during His time on Earth in human form, and letters written to different churches in different regions facing different challenges at/in those different times. The Old Testament is composed of historical events that occurred, prophecies that were communicated, and books of teachings, wisdom, and worship. So, be sure not to allow the "man-made" or "contradictory" misinformed opinions persuade you into thinking that the Bible isn't good for you or isn't for you because a group of people in the past misused it in their attempt to enslave or kill other groups of people. The Bible is for all of us. God is for all of us. Jesus Christ is for all of us.

> *"WHEN FACED WITH A DIFFICULT DECISION OR A QUESTION THAT REQUIRES AN IMMEDIATE RESPONSE ABOUT RIGHT AND WRONG, LET YOUR ANSWER BE SIMPLE >>> IF IT'S NOT FOR GOD, IT'S NOT FOR ME; IF IT'S NOT OF GOD, IT'S NOT OF ME."*
> *[#motivated]*

Friends, there are many people in the world today that are deceived and are deceiving others. Don't blindly follow others because you respect and/or look up to them. Don't let anyone lead you astray or mislead you into accepting sin as the norm. Use the Bible (in its proper context) to measure everything against. If a definition is needed, sin is everything that opposes God. Everything that goes against God, everything that is not for God, and everything that is not of God is sin. Our featured scripture says, "the one who does what is sinful is of the devil, because the devil has been sinning from the beginning. The reason the Son of God appeared was to destroy the devil's work. No one who is born of God will continue to sin, because God's seed remains in them; they cannot go on sinning, because they have been born of God" (1 John 3:8-9, NIV). If you have accepted Jesus Christ into your life as your only Lord and Savior, you have received the truth. You have been given the morals, values, principles, standards, and inner conviction of Jesus Christ via the Holy Spirit. You are a child of light that is called to shine in darkness (John 12:36). You are the righteousness of God (2 Corinthians 5:21). You are the salt of the earth (Matthew 5:13). You are a friend of God (John 15:14). You know what's right and you know what's wrong.

When faced with a difficult decision or a question that requires an immediate response about right and wrong, let your answer be simple >>> if it's not for God, it's not for me; if it's not of God, it's not of me. Make God's ways your ways. Make God's standards your standards. Make God's will your will. Submit completely to Him and commit to living for Him every day of your life and there will be no question about whether you're a true child of God. Just in case you were wondering, no one can have the Father without the Son (you can't accept God without accepting Jesus Christ – 1 John 2:23). The world will be the world, but the children of God must be the children of God. Don't copy the behavior and customs of the world, instead let God transform you into the righteous person that He created you to be by changing the way you think. Then you will know what God's will is for you, which is good, pleasing, and perfect (Romans 12:2). If it's not for God, don't let it be for you!

DEFINE THE PROBLEM | DEVELOP THE SOLUTION

Think about a time that you were influenced by others that did wrong things, and you knew those things were wrong, but you still felt the urge to be influenced by them. It's no coincidence that sin craves more souls to devour, which is why a choice must be made daily to choose God or sin. Confront sin by choosing to stand on the Word of God, which is your foundation. Here's a quick prayer for you, "Father, please help me to always choose You. Although sin and the attractions of the world seem like the best life to have, I know that it's a lie and its destruction disguised as beauty. Help me to not be led by my flesh, but to be always led by You. In Jesus' Name I pray. Amen."

ENCOURAGEMENT OF THE WEEK [#righteous]

To be righteous means to be for God, in God, and with God. God defines the standard criteria and gives it to each of us to measure ourselves against, continuously. Be righteous according to God's definition, not the world's definition.

SPREAD THE MOTIVATION [#motivate]

Encourage someone to look past the glamorous appearance of sin, which is hiding destruction under its appearance. Help them to see the beauty of living for Jesus Christ through the character and conduct that you consistently display.

Week 17 Motivation
IT DOESN'T MATTER!

∞ ∞ ∞

Revelation 3:7 [GNT]
"This is the message from the One who is holy and true. He has the key that belonged to David, and when He opens a door, no one can close it, and when He closes it, no one can open it."

Dear Friends,

Have you ever heard the saying, "What God closes, no one can open, and what God opens, no one can close"? If so, then more than likely the reference came from the featured scripture or Isaiah 22:22, which says, "He will have the keys of office; what he opens, no one will shut, and what he shuts, no one will open" (GNT). The quote is a fact and reminder that God is in complete control. Quick question for you, how much do you care about what others think about you? Be honest! Some of us really care what others think about us, while the rest of us don't really care too much. There isn't a correct way to feel, it's something that we must discuss and work through with God. However, I can tell you that if what others think about you is more important than what God thinks about you, something must change. God's opinion should always matter most. Just like in the featured scripture, which was provided to a specific region of believers called the church of Philadelphia (located in/near modern-day Turkey), God's opinion mattered.

If you're not completely familiar with the book of Revelation, let's quickly go through the basics. While exiled on the island of Patmos for being a proclaimer of the Gospel of Jesus Christ, an angel of Christ was sent to John to reveal events that were to occur. The prophetic message was written in the book of Revelation by John and was to be given to the seven churches in the province of Asia, which were Ephesus, Smyrna, Pergamum, Thyatira, Sardis, Philadelphia, and Laodicea. A specific message was given to each church, addressing some of the things that were going on in that region prior to the numerous prophetic end time events that are also recorded in the book. If we focus on the specific messages for the churches, we'll likely conclude that the message delivered to the church in Philadelphia was probably the most comforting, depending on your outlook. God wanted this group to know that He has an open door for them that no one can shut. The open door represented blessings upon blessings upon blessings in the form of salvation, deliverance, grace, and His covering.

Here's some comforting news for all of us >>> today, that open door still exists, and it extends beyond the region of modern-day Turkey. I'm not sure that you received and fully embraced that good news I just shared, so I'm going to repeat it. Today, that open door still exists, and it extends beyond the region of modern-day Turkey. That means that the open door is extended to you, right now, right where you are. Yes, you! That's a great reason to rejoice and shout with joy, praise, worship, and extreme gratitude to and for God.

"WHEN HE OPENS A DOOR, IT STAYS OPEN UNTIL HE CLOSES IT. WHEN HE CLOSES A DOOR, IT STAYS CLOSED UNTIL HE OPENS IT."
[#motivated]

Friends, here's a public service announcement for you >>> if there is opposition in your life, if there are roadblocks in your life, if there are weapons of all sorts formed against you, it doesn't matter! Did you hear that? I said, it doesn't matter! God is in full control, and He has the final say over every matter, including what happens in your life. When He opens a door, it stays open until He closes it. When He closes a door, it stays closed until He opens it. It's important for us to always remember that. Not sometimes, but all the time! This includes the times when the naysayers give us their unsolicited opinions that God didn't tell them to share with us (#ignoreit). This includes the times when our emotions cause us to second guess the guidance that God provided us (#rejectit). This includes the times when we're tempted to apply logical understanding to God's Word (#overcomeit).

When we experience challenges in our lives, we must not accept the deceptive [misleading, false, dishonest] bait of negative emotions, which can trick us into thinking that God has abandoned us. Learn from the example of the three Hebrew boys (Hananiah/Shadrach, Mishael/Meshach, and Azariah/Abednego in Daniel 3), who trusted God to prevent them from harm, but were prepared to remain committed to Him, even if He didn't spare them from the fire used to threaten their lives. If you're not familiar with that story, grab your bookmark and insert it here (here, meaning this current page in this current book that you're reading), place this book down, and go read Daniel 3, so that you'll know what I'm talking about. We can also learn from the example of the Apostle Paul, who after being bitten by a poisonous viper snake on his journey to Rome (Acts 28), didn't give in to fear, but chose to hold on to the previous word from God that said he would make it to Rome. If you're not familiar with Acts 28 either, grab that bookmark again and redirect your attention to Acts 28. Just in case you misplaced that bookmark or are enjoying this message so much that you don't want to stop reading, I'll give you a quick recap. Paul arrived at an island and started gathering sticks to place on a fire, and as he placed the sticks on the fire, a viper (deadly snake) came out of the heat and latched itself onto Paul's hand. Without extreme panic, Paul shook off the snake into the fire and was unharmed; unharmed like the Hebrew boys in the blazing hot furnace, so be sure to read Acts 28 for the full story.

The point is that it doesn't matter what comes our way during the journey; we must always remember that when God opens the door of blessings, and grace, and mercy, and favor, no one can shut it, no matter how hard they try. We can guarantee that others will try, but it doesn't matter. It doesn't matter! Likewise, when God closes the door on sin and distractions, and removes those sources from our lives, no one can open that door, no matter how hard they try, and they'll try, just as the viper tried to stop Paul from reaching his destination. It doesn't matter! Therefore, let's remember that God holds the key to it all. Anything that opposes God (and His Son Jesus Christ), anything that seeks to break your faith in Him, and anything that seeks to harm you won't matter, can't matter, and doesn't matter, because God said so.

DEFINE THE PROBLEM | DEVELOP THE SOLUTION

Think about a time that you had to make a choice to listen to God and not the people around you. Did that situation end up being better for you or worse after you made the decision to trust God? I think I already know the answer because trusting God will never be the wrong choice. It may seem like a bad decision when the challenges come rushing towards you, but in the end, it will always work out. That's simply because God knows best. Trust Him to do what He always does. Here's a quick prayer for you, "Father, please help me to have the strength and courage to not listen to what other people think or say when it goes against what You want me to do. Help me to not choose others over You. I want to always choose You. You're my God and I live for You. In Jesus' Name I pray. Amen."

ENCOURAGEMENT OF THE WEEK [#confirmed]

When God speaks, we can trust His Word to be the complete truth. There's no need to second guess or add on because His Word is fact. It will always be confirmed because of the Source that it's coming from. He's God! The Creator! So, don't focus on other people's thoughts and opinions, instead always focus on trusting God.

SPREAD THE MOTIVATION [#motivate]

Encourage someone to focus on what God says and think, instead of other people's thoughts and opinions. God will always know what's best for us.

Week 18 Motivation

JUST DO IT!

∞ ∞ ∞

Acts 9:10-16 [NLT]

Now there was a believer in Damascus named Ananias. The Lord spoke to him in a vision, calling, "Ananias!" "Yes, Lord!" he replied. The Lord said, "Go over to Straight Street, to the house of Judas. When you get there, ask for a man from Tarsus named Saul. He is praying to Me right now. I have shown him a vision of a man named Ananias coming in and laying hands on him so he can see again." "But Lord," exclaimed Ananias, "I've heard many people talk about the terrible things this man has done to the believers in Jerusalem! And he is authorized by the leading priests to arrest everyone who calls upon Your Name." But the Lord said, "Go, for Saul is My chosen instrument to take My message to the Gentiles and to kings, as well as to the people of Israel. And I will show him how much he must suffer for My Name's sake."

Dear Friends,

Have you ever received guidance or instructions that sounded like a bad idea from the moment that you received the guidance or instructions? If you answered "yes", then you can relate to Ananias because that's exactly how he felt. Ananias received some very nerve-wracking instructions from Jesus after Jesus appeared to him in a vision (post-resurrection). Jesus wanted Ananias to go and help a man that was widely known for persecuting Jesus-followers (believers). Even more, the man that Ananias was supposed to help had the authority to arrest all Jesus-followers that he came across, and that's exactly what he was doing up until his personal encounter with Jesus that resulted in him losing his sight for three days, along with his strength from not eating or drinking. If we put ourselves in Ananias' position, most of us would think that we didn't hear the instructions too well, right? There's no way that Jesus would send His followers to go help a man that was on an assignment to persecute His followers. That's like volunteering to be slaughtered. If that doesn't highlight the seriousness of the threat, think about an average-sized person challenging a very large grizzly bear to a wrestling match or a person attempting to walk across a swamp filled with very large hungry alligators.

So, Ananias thought similarly to how we would think and decided to tell Jesus what he heard about the man. In other words, Ananias probably thought, "You can't be serious! You want me to go to this terrorist that's looking for people like me to arrest and persecute?!?", but Jesus didn't make a mistake. He knew exactly why Ananias needed to go and He knew what would happen after Ananias went, which is why Jesus responded and said "Go!". In other words, just do it! What can we learn from this story? The first thing we can learn is the Greek word "trelós", which means crazy. Why? Because this is exactly what we would think we were if we heard the instructions that Ananias heard [*insert laughter here*]. What we can really learn is that God knows best. We may not understand His instructions, we may not like His instructions, and we may not want to follow His instructions, but we can trust that God knows best. He has all of the answers, and He knows what's going to happen before it happens. We can trust God to never give us bad guidance or instructions.

> *"WE MAY NOT UNDERSTAND HIS INSTRUCTIONS, WE MAY NOT LIKE HIS INSTRUCTIONS, AND WE MAY NOT WANT TO FOLLOW HIS INSTRUCTIONS, BUT WE CAN TRUST THAT GOD KNOWS BEST."*
> *[#motivated]*

Friends, what instructions have you received from God that you didn't like or fully understand? Did you receive instructions telling you to step out of your comfort zone and take a leap of faith and do something that you normally wouldn't do? Did you receive instructions telling you to believe that God can produce the miracle that no one thinks is possible? Did you receive instructions telling you to be still and do nothing, even though you feel compelled [forced obligated] to do something? If you answered "yes" to any of these scenarios, know that you're not alone. Ananias wasn't alone when he received his instructions, and neither are you. If you're wondering about the ending of this story, Ananias went to the man and restored his sight, and that same man ended up being considered one of the most polarizing and controversial Jesus-followers in history because he went from persecuting Jesus-followers to becoming one of the greatest Jesus-followers that ever lived. That man was the Apostle Paul, the author of several books (or letters/epistles) of the New Testament. What if Ananias disobeyed the instructions of Jesus and never went to the man because of the fear that he felt? It's possible that we wouldn't have a New Testament to study; it's possible that the gospel of Jesus Christ would not have been preached to us; and it's possible that none of us would have a relationship with Jesus Christ as a result.

Do you understand the significance of this event? This is why we must follow God's instructions when He gives them to us. We won't know how everything connects, we won't know who will be impacted, and we won't know the specific outcomes of our obedience. We must simply listen and obey. Just do it! Ananias told Jesus what he heard, and Jesus told him to "go!", which can be another way of saying, just do it! That's His advice to us today. Don't tell God what you heard, listen to what He said. Just do it! So, whatever you're being instructed to do, understand that God has a specific purpose and reason for it. All you have to do is let go of your rationale and reasoning, and trust God with all your heart. Just do it!

DEFINE THE PROBLEM | DEVELOP THE SOLUTION

Think about a time that you decided not to listen to God's instructions. What happened because of your disobedience? Was it worth it? Of course not! Nothing is worth our relationship with God. Disobedience to His instructions can lead to very bad decisions and very bad results. Always yield to His guidance, directions, and instructions because He knows best. He's God! Here's a quick prayer for you, "Father, please help me to be humble enough to acknowledge that I don't have all of the answers, but You do. Help me to accept Your corrections and guidance in life and help me to respectfully keep Your commands and follow Your instructions, always. In Jesus' Name I pray. Amen."

ENCOURAGEMENT OF THE WEEK [#obedience]

To obey God is to humbly accept His commands, guidance, directions, and instructions, and live according to His will. Obedience leaves no room for additional solutions or discretion. When we choose to obey God, we give Him our will in exchange for His.

SPREAD THE MOTIVATION [#motivate]

Encourage someone to accept God's correction because He corrects those that He loves. Let them know that God loves them, despite their flaws.

Week 19 Motivation
PURPOSEFUL PAIN

∞ ∞ ∞

2 Corinthians 7:10-11 [CJB]

Pain handled in God's way produces a turning from sin to God which leads to salvation, and there is nothing to regret in that! But pain handled in the world's way produces only death. For just look at what handling the pain God's way produced in you! What earnest diligence, what eagerness to clear yourselves, what indignation, what fear, what longing, what zeal, what readiness to put things right! In everything you have proved yourselves blameless in the matter.

Dear Friends,

Have you ever experienced pain? If you had the choice to eliminate all pain from your life completely, would you choose to do so? No matter what we prefer, pain has essentially become a normal part of life. We experience different types of pain. Pain occurs during times of distress, times of injury, times of grief, times of sorrow, and the list goes on and on. No matter what type of pain it is, it's fair to state that all pain produces a level of unpleasant discomfort and hurt that many of us would avoid if we were given the choice to avoid or keep it. While there are many types of pain, let's focus this message on the pain that occurs because of our bad decisions, since this is the point of the featured scripture. Have you ever made a bad decision and had to live with the adverse consequences [results, effects] that resulted from your bad decision? As you think about some of your past bad decisions, I'll share one of my bad decisions with you.

> *"Once upon a time I really enjoyed playing basketball (when I had more hair and youthful legs), so I went to the gym to play a pickup game of full-court basketball. I knew I was going to have a good game because I was feeling good. Real good. Good like leather pants in the 1980s [insert laughter here]. Well, on the first play of the game, I sprained my right ankle. It was the very first play. I couldn't just stop playing after I was so pumped up to play, which is what I thought to myself in those immediate seconds following the sprain. I decided to simply tie my sneaker a little tighter and I kept playing because that's what we did back then, right? The adrenaline was going, so I was able to finish the game. I played well and won, so I decided to play a few more games (still with the sprained ankle). Again, the adrenaline was going (you can see this is a bad decision, right?), and I endured the pain throughout each game, but then the last game was over. The adrenaline had decreased, and the reality of this severely sprained ankle had set in. Over the next*

few hours following that last basketball game, my ankle had doubled in size, was bright red, my ability to walk was very impaired, my ability to drive was very limited because it was my right ankle, I was unable to sleep because of the intense ankle pain, and as an added bonus, a random charley horse (cramp) just happened to occur in the same leg around 2 a.m. Fast-forward a few hours later, the local hospital revealed that I had a very bad fractured ankle, which likely worsened as I continued to play. Bad decision, right?"

If given the time, I'm sure that we all can think about some of our past bad decisions that resulted in some form of pain. Keep in mind, there are two ways to handle pain, as noted in the featured scripture. There's God's way, which produces a turning from sin to God and leads to salvation; and then there's the world's way, which produces only death. Depending on which way we decide to go, pain can either be used as a teacher of an important life lesson or a warning that's ignored.

"HE ALLOWS US TO EXPERIENCE PURPOSEFUL PAIN TO HELP REDIRECT OUR FOCUS AND REVIVE OUR FAITH IN HIM, WHILE HELPING US BUILD CHARACTER IN THE PROCESS."
[#motivate]

Friends, are you aware that every action has a consequence? It's the common cause and effect scenario – the result is caused by the action. Are you also aware of the importance of discipline and correction, which is often used to introduce a level of unpleasant discomfort (or pain) to help us avoid making the same bad decisions. Proverbs 3:11-12 says, "Don't reject the LORD's discipline, and don't be upset when He corrects you. For the LORD corrects those He loves, just as a father corrects a child in whom he delights" (NLT). Consider discipline or purposeful pain as a means for God to get our attention because of His immeasurable [endless, unlimited] love for us. What is this purposeful pain that was just mentioned? It's the type of pain that motivates us to turn to God, especially after our unhealthy and abusive relationship with sin causes us to continue to make bad decisions. Yes, any type of relationship with sin will be unhealthy and abusive because we'll be battered, destroyed, and weakened spiritually (and physically at times) with sin at the helm. But God!

God provides us a way or a path to get back on track with Him. He allows us to experience purposeful pain to help redirect our focus and revive our faith in Him, while helping us build character in the process. Keep in mind, His mercy prevents us from experiencing the full amount of pain and punishment that our actions deserve. None of us deserve God's forgiveness or the many second chances that He gives us after we continue to make repeated mistakes, but His love for us is immeasurable and we become super blessed recipients of His unexplainable grace and mercy. Therefore, don't choose to ignore the warnings and handle pain according to the world's way.

Instead, choose God's way, and grab a hold of Jesus Christ and never let go. Allow the purposeful pain to lead you directly to Him, which will lead you to salvation. There is nothing to regret in that.

DEFINE THE PROBLEM | DEVELOP THE SOLUTION

Think about a time that you made a bad decision, and the decision ended up helping you learn what not to do and what to do in future similar situations. That's an example of pain that ended up being purposeful because of God's grace and mercy. Always choose to look at the opportunity to learn from the experiences. Here's a quick prayer for you, "Father, please help me to continue to be teachable and accept Your correction. Help me to maintain a humble heart that is willingly obedient to You. Allow me to learn from the experiences that You allow me to go through, knowing that You are always with me. In Jesus' Name I pray. Amen."

ENCOURAGEMENT OF THE WEEK [#teachable]

To truly learn, we must be teachable. Being teachable means possessing a level of humility, while acknowledging that we don't have all of the answers and need to be taught. God often uses our experiences to teach us, including the experiences that result from the decisions that we make. If we're open to His teaching and correction, He'll allow us to be open to His rewards.

SPREAD THE MOTIVATION [#motivate]

Encourage someone to admit that none of us have all of the answers in life and let them know that it's okay to not be perfect or all-knowing. God is! God allows each of us to learn from Him.

Week 20 Motivation

TUNE OUT THE NOISE

∞ ∞ ∞

Matthew 4:8-11 [NIV]

Again, the devil took Him to a very high mountain and showed Him all the kingdoms of the world and their splendor. "All this I will give You," he said, "if You will bow down and worship me." Jesus said to him, "Away from Me, Satan! For it is written: 'Worship the LORD your God, and serve Him only.'" Then the devil left Him, and angels came and attended Him.

Dear Friends,

Have you ever been exposed to an unpleasant sound or disturbing noise? Think beyond the many lectures that you received when you were younger about your tendency to leave crumbs in the butter, or your inexcusable habit of only leaving a few drops of milk in the container that's in the refrigerator, perfectly in place to appear as a full container of milk ready for someone else to use, only for that someone to be disappointed after grabbing the empty milk container (maybe I'm reminiscing too much) [*insert laughter here*]. When we're presented with disturbing noise, our natural reaction is to tune it out, just like you did when you had that five-minute lecture about milk. This is what Jesus did as the devil was attempting to tempt Him with the "flesh-enticers". What are the "flesh-enticers"? It's a made-up term that sounds like it should be included in every sermon, every intellectual social media post, and every time you feel like impressing others with intellectual words that are completely irrelevant to the conversation. So, go ahead and include it in your next speech, and let me know how well it worked out for you [*insert laughter here*]. Flesh-enticers are the things that entice [attract, tempt, lure] the flesh, but lead us further away from God.

As we read in the featured scripture, the devil's final attempt was to try to lure Jesus away from God by enticing His flesh with wealth and power, but it conflicted with God's plan. Since it conflicted with God's plan, it had no room in Jesus' life. The devil was quickly rebuked and rejected, and his failed attempt was equivalent [equal, comparable, same as] to disturbing noise. Jesus provided us with an example of how to tune out the noise.

"EVERYTHING THAT CONFLICTS WITH GOD'S WORD IS EQUIVALENT TO DISTURBING NOISE."
[#motivated]

Friends, God's Word is the standard. This is where we say "period!". You know when people really want to emphasize their point and say "period!" after the strong point was made that shifted the argument in their favor? Well, this is one of those times, so join me right now in saying "period!". Everything that conflicts with God's Word is equivalent to disturbing noise. It's imperative [very important] that we follow Jesus' example and tune out the noise. Our faith, hope, and trust in God is formed because of us believing His Word to be true. He notified us in Isaiah 55:11 that His Word will not return to Him empty, but will accomplish the purpose for which He sent it. In other words, if God said it will happen, it will happen ("period!"). It's also important to remember that temptations often occur when we're standing on faith or are making strides in the right direction. It's true, think about it. Reflect on a time that you were trusting God to help you get over bad money management habits. If this has never happened to you because you've always been excellent at managing money, think about someone that this has happened to. You may have created a budget and kept up with it, and was doing very well for a few weeks, but just when you thought that you had the bad habit conquered, those new clothes went on sale and called your name from the store, or that discounted vacation trip whispered in your ear as you saw the advertisement, or that meal from that expensive restaurant sent its aroma to your nose as you walked past it. Whatever it was, it was something sent your way to lure you away from the deliverance that you had been experiencing. Get the point?

Temptations often present us with alternative [other, different] options that conflict with God's instructions for us. The "flesh-enticers" are sent our way to break our faith in God and redirect that same faith away from God and towards "others". FYI, the "others" category is broad and includes things and people. Guess what? When those "flesh-enticers" appear, we can do what Jesus did and tune out the disturbing noise. Don't entertain the noise, tune it out and continue to trust God! If you've been allowing those "flesh-enticers" to influence your life somehow, someway, then more than likely, you've been drifting away from God. Drift no longer, drift no further! Instead, follow Jesus' example and tune out the disturbing noise. All of it! If we resist the devil, he will flee from us (repeat that line a few times and replace "we" with "I"). Let's continue to stand on faith, despite what happens around us, and let's always remember to tune out the noise.

DEFINE THE PROBLEM | DEVELOP THE SOLUTION

Think about a time that you had to tune out noise to focus. Were you successful? If so, continue to build on that, especially as it pertains to opposition of God's Word. Don't lend an attentive ear to the noise; block it out and remain focused on your relationship with God. Here's a quick prayer for you, "Father, please help me to not allow temptation, manipulation, or deception to interfere with my relationship with You. Help me to discern and block out all noise from entering my life. I choose You, always. In Jesus' Name I pray. Amen."

ENCOURAGEMENT OF THE WEEK [#period]

A period used in a sentence is an indicator that the sentence is complete. That's exactly how we should treat God's Word because it's complete and final. It doesn't matter what noise is being discussed around us, God's Word is final. Remember that as you resist temptation designed to knock you off track.

SPREAD THE MOTIVATION [#motivate]

Encourage someone to tune out the noise and all of the distractions by focusing on God and not others.

Week 21 Motivation

NAVIGATING INEVITABLE ADVERSITY

∞ ∞ ∞

James 1:2-4 [NIV]
Consider it pure joy, my brothers and sisters, whenever you face trials of many kinds, because you know that the testing of your faith produces perseverance. Let perseverance finish its work so that you may be mature and complete, not lacking anything.

Dear Friends,

If you were asked to describe how you handle adversity, what would your response be? In other words, how well do you deal with problems that you're confronted by? If a definition of adversity is needed, it can be defined as an adverse or unfortunate event or circumstance (think in terms of difficulty). Adversity is generally experienced in the form of problems, challenges, tests, trials, tribulations, hardships, misfortune, periods of loss, and other types of difficulty. Doesn't sound too thrilling, right? That's because adversity causes discomfort. Not the type of discomfort that you may feel when another driver decides to move in front of you at the most inconvenient time possible, or the discomfort that you may feel when you hold the door open for someone that's too busy to say, "thank you!". That type of discomfort may be called an annoyance that you'll get through with the help of much needed prayer [*insert laughter here*]. You may have heard the saying, "be comfortable being uncomfortable" or "be comfortable in discomfort", but that's one of those sayings that we really don't want to hear while we're going through difficult times. I'm almost certain that you've witnessed people not wanting to hear encouraging scriptures while they're going through extreme difficulty, right? That's because challenges are designed to draw out what's deep inside of the heart. That means, we get to find out what our character truly is when we're confronted by problems. We can either break or stand strong; trust God or accept doubt; be encouraged by His promises or be discouraged by the occurrences.

As followers of Jesus Christ, we've been given certain assurances. We've already been assured that we'll experience adversity in life (John 16:33). We've already been assured that the world will not accept us and may hate us because the world didn't accept Jesus and hated Him (John 15:18-21). We've already been assured that we are recipients of God's grace (John 1:16). We've also been assured that God gives us victory through Jesus Christ (1 Corinthians 15:57). Did you hear that? We have victory through Jesus Christ. This is the reason for the joy that's mentioned in the featured scripture. The result has already been determined. Yes, it's true that adversity is an inevitable [expected, unavoidable] experience that each of us must go through, no matter how old, how young, how wealthy, how poor, how wise, or how foolish we are. No one is exempt. If anyone tells you differently, I recommend that you reject it to avoid being deceived and let down. However, there's good news found in the Good News (Good News is another term for the Gospel of Jesus Christ). Peace, perseverance, character, and hope are some of things that we can look forward to (Romans 5:1-5).

"WE CAN EITHER BREAK OR STAND STRONG; TRUST GOD OR ACCEPT DOUBT; BE ENCOURAGED BY HIS PROMISES OR BE DISCOURAGED BY THE OCCURRENCES."
[#motivated]

Friends, as referenced earlier, in John 16:33, Jesus said, "In this world you will have trouble" (NIV), which is another way of saying that we will experience adversity. Notice that Jesus didn't say that we may experience adversity or that adversity is a possibility, He said we will. But, if we keep reading, we'll see that He instructs us to take heart [be brave] because He has overcome [conquered] the world. In other words, don't be afraid of the adversity when it confronts you, keep trusting God and stand on the Good News of Jesus Christ. When the challenges associated with your household, relationships, careers, or anything else that's important to you, attempt to knock you off balance, don't give in to the fear or stress that it wants you to accept. Instead, take heart and be brave, and know that God has you covered. Yes, God has you covered.

The featured scripture says, consider it pure joy whenever you face the different kinds of trials [adversity] because it will produce perseverance and endurance. Many people often use endurance and perseverance interchangeably, but for the purposes of this message we're going to disjoin them and say endurance is the ability to endure or withstand adversity, and perseverance is the ability to overcome or get through adversity. Both endurance and perseverance come from God because of our right standing with Jesus Christ. That means if you want to navigate adversity successfully, you'll need the endurance and perseverance that Jesus offers us. He allows us to be equipped with the strength to withstand and overcome. He enables us the ability to keep on pushing and progressing no matter what obstacles are sent our way. He gives us the hope we need.

Therefore, consider it pure joy when adversity comes your way because adversity will be joined by God's grace, wrapped in endurance and perseverance, which will make us complete, whole, and mature in faith. So, be filled with joy and don't lose hope as you navigate adversity with Jesus by your side every step of the way. Let's continue to endure and persevere through it all.

DEFINE THE PROBLEM | DEVELOP THE SOLUTION

Think about a time that you went through a major form of adversity. You're still here today, so that means you survived it. It may have left wounds or scars, but you're still here. Use that testimony to fuel and recharge your faith in God each day, as you partner with the Savior Jesus Christ. Here's a quick prayer for you, "Father, please help me to always remain in right standing with You. Help me to never give up or surrender to the adversity that I face. Instead, help me to grow from each challenge and learn the valuable lessons that I must learn to be a better representative of Jesus Christ. In Jesus' Name I pray. Amen."

ENCOURAGEMENT OF THE WEEK [#adversity]

Adversity can occur in different forms of challenges, but it can also provide different benefits. Lessons are learned through experiences, and sometimes the lessons that we must learn are taught through the adverse experiences that we go through. The good news is that we'll never be alone because God has given us a Savior in Jesus Christ that is always with us because of our faith in Him. Let your faith in Him grow stronger each day.

SPREAD THE MOTIVATION [#motivate]

Encourage someone to stand strong amid the difficulty. When God is the foundation, we're guaranteed to survive the storm and can consider it a test that we'll pass because of His love for us.

Week 22 Motivation

NAVIGATING INEVITABLE ADVERSITY (PART II)

∞ ∞ ∞

James 2:14 [CJB]
What good is it, my brothers, if someone claims to have faith but has no actions to prove it? Is such "faith" able to save him?

Dear Friends,

Is it possible to see faith? If so, what does faith look like? Keep that question in mind as we discuss adversity. As we learned in the previous message, adversity can be defined as an adverse or unfortunate event or circumstance (think in terms of difficulty) and is generally experienced in the form of problems, challenges, tests, trials, tribulations, hardships, misfortune, periods of loss, and other types of difficulty. Adversity is inevitable, meaning it's unavoidable. We will, at different points in our lives, experience adversity. Maybe the adversity will come in the form of losing a fourth grade spelling bee contest because someone didn't remember that "committee" was one of those words with extra letters for no apparent reason (as you can tell, I still haven't forgotten about that spelling bee loss I suffered in the fourth grade) [*insert laughter here*]. The point is, whether it's a spelling bee loss or something else, we will experience different forms of adversity. It's important to note that the adversity that we experience isn't as important and vital as our response to adversity. Sure, it may seem as if the storm that you're going through is the most difficult time that you've ever faced and you're praying that God takes it away from you as soon as possible, but God's paying more attention to how you react to the storm. He knows what the storm can and can't do. The storm has limitations set by God.

Sometimes, we must go through these different types of adversity to advance to the next level. If you need specific examples, God tested Abraham (Genesis 22:1) and He tested the Israelites many times (Exodus 15:25; Exodus 16:4; Judges 3:1). Keep in mind, the presence or absence of faith is one of the primary factors that separate true followers of Jesus from lukewarm followers of Jesus. If you would like to know how God feels about lukewarm followers, look at Revelation 3:15-16. If Jesus is an active presence in your life, your faith in Him must not be dependent on what's happening around you. Instead, it should be unwavering, unconditional, and operational [fully working] at all times. If we want to take it a step further, our faith should be seen. How can faith be seen? Great question! According to the featured scripture, faith must produce action. In other words, our faith is expressed and seen through our actions. What happens when we navigate adversity with faith?

"CONSIDER EVERY PROBLEM, EVERY CHALLENGE, EVERY OBSTACLE, EVERY TRIAL, EVERY STORM, AND EVERY DIFFICULTY AS AN OPPORTUNITY AND A MEANS TO GROW IN FAITH AND ADVANCE TO THE NEXT LEVEL IN CHRIST."
[#motivate]

Friends, when we navigate adversity with faith, we refuse to allow our circumstances to dictate our response. Sure, the challenges will be difficult at times, but challenges were never designed to be very easy. Challenges are designed to test endurance and produce perseverance. Good news! We don't just have ordinary endurance; we have the endurance that comes from Jesus Christ. The same endurance that allowed Jesus to withstand crucifixion, persecution, and even death on a cross. It doesn't stop there. We have the same endurance that activated Jesus' perseverance, which allowed Him to conquer death, sin, evil, darkness, curses, and everything that attempts to oppose God. We are heavily equipped! Your response begins in your heart and mind. Remind yourself of the endurance that has been made available to you through Jesus Christ, and let it produce within you the faith, trust, belief, and hope needed to confront every form of adversity that comes knocking at your door. Remember, challenges are not meant to destroy you, but test you.

Therefore, consider every problem, every challenge, every obstacle, every trial, every storm, and every difficulty as an opportunity and a means to grow in faith and advance to the next level in Christ. You're an overcomer, a super conqueror, and a son/daughter of God, because of your relationship with Jesus Christ. With this in mind, let's choose to navigate the inevitable adversity with unwavering faith in Christ, which will ultimately result in us being fully equipped with His endurance and perseverance.

DEFINE THE PROBLEM | DEVELOP THE SOLUTION

Think about a time when you were very confident in a skill or ability that you had. You were so confident that you knew you were going to succeed. Your unwavering faith is a similar skill and ability that should prompt confidence. With unwavering faith in Jesus Christ, we're guaranteed to succeed in God's eyes because we're opening our complete heart to Him and trusting Him to lead, guide, and direct us. This is what God wants us to do, so let's keep doing it. Here's a quick prayer for you, "Father, please help me to maintain unwavering faith in You and in my Lord and Savior Jesus Christ. Help me to not give up when challenges arise; help me to not give in to temptation and take short cuts that are not directed by You and help me to remain disciplined in my commitment to You. Whenever I'm tempted to accept disbelief and doubt, help me to be reminded of the previous success that You allowed me to have because of Your great love for me. In Jesus' Name I pray. Amen."

ENCOURAGEMENT OF THE WEEK [#unwavering]

When something is unwavering, it is firm, solid, and persistent. That's how our faith in Jesus Christ must be. Unwavering faith isn't faith that falters or withers away when adversity appears. It's the type of faith that is anchored deep within and provides a foundational level of comfort because the faith is placed in the best Source possible, Jesus Christ the Savior. We were created to have unwavering faith, so let's keep it.

SPREAD THE MOTIVATION [#motivate]

Encourage someone to simply trust God. To let go of the control, to let go of the baggage, to let go of the plans, and trust in His will and His plan.

Week 23 Motivation

MORE THAN ENOUGH

∞ ∞ ∞

Matthew 15:35-38 [GNT]

So, Jesus ordered the crowd to sit down on the ground. Then He took the seven loaves and the fish, gave thanks to God, broke them, and gave them to the disciples; and the disciples gave them to the people. They all ate and had enough. Then the disciples took up seven baskets full of pieces left over. The number of men who ate was four thousand, not counting the women and children.

Dear Friends,

    Have you ever experienced lack or shortage? If the answer is yes, I think we can all agree that if given the choice we'd choose to have more than enough instead of not enough, right? If we focus on the featured scripture, we'll notice that not enough was converted [changed, transformed] to more than enough by Jesus. Many people had been with Jesus for three days and it was time for them to part ways, but Jesus had compassion for them and didn't want any of them to possibly collapse on the journey home due to hunger, since they had not eaten for an extended period (is there anything greater than a compassionate Savior?). However, there was a major problem. There were only seven loaves of bread, a few fish, and over four thousand people. Yes, you heard that correctly. Seven loaves of bread and a few fish; not a lot of fish, a very small number of fish.

    I think we'll all arrive at the same conclusion that there wasn't enough food to feed over four thousand people, but God! It's hard to express how big of a deal this was, so let's try. Think about a very, very large church gathering with very, very hungry churchgoers (the ones that get very grumpy and disturbed when they're hungry and the service exceeds the normal time), and only five plates of food available to feed all of those very, very hungry people (uh-oh!). Let's get back to the story. The disciples were about to learn a very valuable lesson – nothing is impossible for God. He's the Way Maker when there's no way. He's the Provider when there's drought. He's the Miracle Worker when impossibility surrounds us. Jesus gave thanks to the Father, broke the food, gave the food to the disciples, and the disciples provided the food to the people. After everyone had eaten enough, the disciples collected seven large baskets of leftover pieces of food. In case you missed it the first time, Jesus converted not enough to more than enough. FYI, this is the perfect time to say, "Won't He do it?!".

*"**Nothing is impossible for God. He's the Way Maker when there's no way out; He's the Provider when there's drought; He's the Miracle Worker when impossibility surrounds us.**"*
[#motivated]

Friends, notice the sequence of events that occurred >>> (1) Jesus gave thanks to God and essentially blessed the food; (2) broke the food, multiplying what was at hand; (3) equipped the disciples to be in a position to share with the people; (4) enabled the disciples to feed the large number of people; and (5) the people that didn't have enough ended up having more than enough through Jesus. So, what can we learn from this? If we were to dive deeper, we would notice that everything - every blessing, every miracle, every supernatural experience in our lives, will always begin with praising and thanking God. When we start with God, we start with the Source and Creator of life. He'll take the little in our lives and multiply it, not so that we can keep everything for ourselves, but so that we may be equipped to share with His people that are in need. In the end, everyone can witness for themselves that God is more than enough. His love, His grace, His mercy, His peace, His comfort, and His favor are more than enough.

Therefore, it doesn't matter what situations we face in life, if Jesus Christ is in the mix, the battle is fixed for us to overcome. We overcome everything through Jesus Christ, the Alpha and the Omega (the 'A' and the 'Z'), the First and the Last, the Beginning and the End. We overcome because we rely and depend on the Creator, not the created. FYI, depending on the created instead of the Creator opens the door to idolatry. No longer shall we allow those trying times that we experience to occupy our minds and weigh heavy on our heart. Let's turn to the Way Maker and watch Him provide the way. He's more than enough!

Define the Problem | Develop the Solution

Think about a time that you were unsure of how you were going to pay that bill or get by without enough money, but God turned the not enough into more than enough. It bypassed just enough and went directly to more than enough. How do I know that? Because you're still standing in victory. Maybe you haven't experienced the full extent of the victory yet, but that doesn't change the fact that you're the recipient of more than enough. Trust God to reveal it to you. Here's a quick prayer for you, "Father, please help me to rely on You, rather than rely on people or things to meet my needs. You know exactly what I need and when I need it. Help me to remember to simply trust You to provide. In Jesus' Name I pray. Amen."

ENCOURAGEMENT OF THE WEEK [#overcomer]

An overcomer is a person that overcomes a difficult situation. Overcomer and success are synonymous with one another because an overcomer is guaranteed to succeed. What makes us overcomers? Not ourselves, but God! The presence of God through the active presence of Jesus Christ in our lives causes us to overcome difficulty.

SPREAD THE MOTIVATION [#motivate]

Encourage someone to not look at the glass as half empty, but to see the potential of the glass being almost full. (FYI – the glass is a metaphor for anything that is half of its whole).

Week 24 Motivation

IT'S NOT OVER!

∞ ∞ ∞

John 2:18-22 [NIV]

The Jews then responded to Him, "What sign can You show us to prove Your authority to do all this?" Jesus answered them, "Destroy this Temple, and I will raise it again in three days." They replied, "It has taken forty-six years to build this temple, and You are going to raise it in three days?" But the Temple He had spoken of was His Body. After He was raised from the dead, His disciples recalled what He had said. Then they believed the scripture and the words that Jesus had spoken.

Dear Friends,

It's not over! What do you think about when you hear that statement? That's the title and focus of this message, and it'll be emphasized throughout this message because it's important for us to know that (it's not over!). Yes, you read that correctly, (it's not over!). Now, let's go back many, many, many years ago, when Jesus was fed up and had enough of people selling different goods [animals for sacrifice] in the temple courts in Israel. So, what did Jesus do as He saw merchants selling cattle, sheep, and doves for sacrifices, and dealers at tables exchanging foreign currency? He made a whip from some ropes and chased them all out of the temple, essentially clearing the temple courts of the reckless and meaningless retail behavior. "He drove out the sheep and cattle, scattered the money changers' coins over the floor, and turned over their tables. Then, going over to the people who sold doves, he told them, 'Get these things out of here. Stop turning my Father's house into a marketplace!'" (John 2:15-16, GNT). FYI, sacrifice that's not from the heart is meaningless, which means purchasing damaged goods at the last minute to give to God isn't the type of meaningful sacrifice that He's well-pleased with

As expected, people were upset with Jesus, so they asked Him to prove His authority. Jesus answered with a very significant response, and said "Destroy this temple, and I will raise it again in three days". The people thought that Jesus had lost His mind [gone crazy, was mentally unstable]. There's no way that a temple that took forty-six years to build was going to be destroyed and rebuilt by Him in three days. Sounds impossible just thinking about it, right? If you're not aware of the full story, it's greater than what it seemed. Jesus wasn't talking about the actual temple, He was referring to the Temple that houses the Holy Spirit, the Temple that is greater than any physical building, the Temple that God always filled with His presence. The Temple that He was referring to was His body.

Remember, the body is referred to as the temple of the Holy Spirit (1 Corinthians 6:19). Jesus was giving the people an advanced notice of what would occur – ultimate victory over everything. (It's not over!). Over the next few days, Jesus would be arrested, accused, mocked, mistreated, crucified on a cross, and buried in a tomb that was sealed with a huge stone, but (it's not over!). What happened next? Jesus, after having His Temple destroyed, raised it again in three days. Recall what He told the people days before. He did exactly what He said He would do and ultimately proved His authority to death, sin, evil, disease, sickness, illness, pride, rebellion, and everything else that attempts to come against God.

"RESURRECTION OCCURS WHEN REVIVAL, REBIRTH, RESTORATION, AND RESURGENCE OCCUR. RESURRECTION OCCURS WHEN DEATH IS CONFRONTED BY LIFE."
[#motivated]

Friends, what can we learn from this very important event in history? It's not over! Yes, indeed, it's not over! The current tense ("it's") is intentional because the resurrection and victory that Jesus enabled wasn't limited to a single day in Israel many, many, many years ago. That day of victory continues today. The resurrection is still occurring today. Resurrection occurs when revival, rebirth, restoration, and resurgence occur. Resurrection occurs when death is confronted by life; when life gives death a reminder that life will always be greater than death.

With all that's going on in the world these days, it's important to know that (it's not over!). Many people are battling different things, but (it's not over!). Many people are on the verge of losing everything of value, but (it's not over!). Many people are lost, helpless, hopeless, and confused, but (it's not over!). It's not over until God says it's over. If God isn't giving up, we don't have permission to give up. We cannot give up. Death has no power over life. So, let's live because Jesus Christ lives. The resurrection of Jesus is the victory for us. Anyone that chooses to believe that Jesus Christ is the Resurrected Lord and Savior and chooses to live a life submitted to Him is guaranteed victory. Nothing can overtake you and nothing can overcome you. If God is for you, there is nothing that can come against you and prevail. Death had a temporary victory, but God! God reminded everyone and everything that He's in complete control. The resurrection of Jesus is equivalent to ultimate victory. We have ultimate victory today and forever through Jesus Christ. When our lives on earth are over, we'll live in the presence of God and our Savior Jesus Christ forever. That's victory! Ultimate victory! So, no matter what you're going through at this present time, know that (it's not over!). The resurrection applies to each situation. Be revived, rebirthed, restored, and resurged in faith, in hope, in life, in health, and in all things because (it's not over!).

DEFINE THE PROBLEM | DEVELOP THE SOLUTION

Think about a time that you were losing a battle, any battle, and it seemed as if you were done, and the battle was lost. There was no path to victory for you. It was clear that you were going to be defeated in this battle, but just when you accepted that you were going to lose, God stepped in and changed everything in an instant. How did you feel? Remember that feeling and carry the feeling for the remainder of your life, as You trust God every day. Here's a quick prayer for you, "Father, please help me to trust You in every situation and in every matter. Help me to know that You have the final say and nothing is over until You say it's over. Help me to remember that I have victory through the Savior Jesus Christ. In Jesus' Name I pray. Amen."

ENCOURAGEMENT OF THE WEEK [#victory]

Victory is a very important word for every believer and follower of Jesus Christ. Why? Because it's what we have! It's in our born-again DNA because it's in the blood of Christ. Jesus has victory over everything that seeks to come against God, which means through the blood of Christ, we have victory over everything that seeks to come against God. Walk victory, talk victory, and live victory through Jesus Christ.

SPREAD THE MOTIVATION [#motivate]

Encourage a brother/sister to remember that victory isn't based on the opponent, it's guaranteed, despite the opponent. The blood of Jesus Christ prevails, always.

Week 25 Motivation
GIVE IT TO GOD

∞ ∞ ∞

Psalm 68:19-20 [GNT]
Praise the Lord, who carries our burdens day after day; He is the God who saves us. Our God is a God who saves; He is the LORD, our Lord, who rescues us from death.

Dear Friends,

Are you currently carrying any burdens? If so, I want you to know that there's Someone that cares about your burdens and cares about you as well. Here's something that I'm sure you already knew >>> we'll all endure different challenges throughout the course of our lives. When I say challenges, think bigger than that time you spent an hour at the grocery store filling up the shopping cart with items to purchase, only to realize that you left your money at home, as you began to think about possible ways that you can recover that one hour that you won't get back during your grocery-less drive home (this may or may not have happened to me). Then you thought about a positive (+) coming out of this negative (-) situation, which was that you didn't have to spend a lot of time searching for the groceries when you returned to the store because you knew where to find everything, as you checked your wallet multiples times to make sure you had your money this time [*insert laughter here*]. Think about your current life and all of its baggage. We've already endured a few challenges. If you're still here and able to read this message or listen to this message, that means you've persevered [continued, didn't stop]. In other words, those challenges that you experienced did not end you. You're still standing, still living, still breathing, and now you must ensure you're still praising. Why? Because of God!

The LORD has allowed us to make it through all of those tough times and difficult periods. If we're unwise in our thinking, we'll attribute it [give credit] to our relentless will and ambition [drive, determination], but it's important for us to remember that God will always have the final say. That means you can do everything right according to your plan, but if God doesn't want your plan to be carried out, it won't be carried out. A lot of times, it's for our benefit. We have a God that always has our best interest in mind, which means He'll provide us guidance and direction to help keep us away from self-destruction. We must listen to Him. (Let's repeat that). We must listen to Him.

The featured scripture says, "Our God is a God who saves". Let's meditate [think, reflect] on that one for a few minutes. This means that all of those bad choices and bad decisions we've made that should've ended us, did not because we have a God who saves. All of those times that we found ourselves in the middle of terrifying storms [hard times] that were designed to break us or end our lives, did not and could not because we have a God who saves.

"As long as you're able to breathe, you're able to be reconciled to God through Jesus Christ. God's love is greater than our sin."
[#motivated]

Friends, it doesn't matter what you've been through or what you're going through, you must give it to God. It's just that simple. Give God those past mistakes, the current mistakes, the guilt, the shame, the regret, and the feelings of unworthiness. Don't be deceived into thinking that your previous or current lifestyle is too sinful for God to forgive. As long as you're able to breathe, you're able to be reconciled to God through Jesus Christ. God's love is greater than our sin. Do you understand that? God's love is greater than our sin (repeat that to yourself a few more times). From the Sovereign LORD comes escape from death, which means salvation, deliverance, and eternal life with Him occurs because of our relationship with Him. Keep in mind, this doesn't mean that we'll be exempt [excused, freed] from challenges. We can be certain that there will be tests, trials, and faith-building experiences that occur in our lives. We can also be certain that we'll be prepared for it all. Just as Joseph was prepared for the drought (Genesis 41). Just as Joshua was prepared for battle (book of Joshua). We will also be prepared because our God is a God that saves. What should we do now?

Before doing anything, we must make sure we're in right standing with God. This means that we must humble ourselves and repent. We must acknowledge our wrong behavior, acknowledge that a change must take place, seek God's forgiveness, and change the behavior. Forgiving ourselves is a crucial part of the sequence of events as well, so if you're holding on to any form of "self-unforgiveness", let it go! We must not allow guilt and regret to lead us back to hopelessness and feelings of unworthiness. The truth is, we're all unworthy, we've all sinned multiple times, But God! Our God is a God that saves. After we've humbled ourselves, repented, and rejected all of those deceiving feelings, we must trust God every step of the way. We must submit and commit to God. After that, it doesn't matter what comes our way, we'll be ready, willing, and able to give it to God.

DEFINE THE PROBLEM | DEVELOP THE SOLUTION

Think about a time that you carried baggage. Maybe you didn't know that you were carrying it for so long or maybe you were fully aware. What happened when you got rid of the baggage and no longer carried it? Wasn't there relief? That relief should be felt each day. Don't continue to carry baggage that Jesus Christ wants to take from you. He wants to lift the heavy burdens from each of us, so let Him. Here's a quick prayer for you, "Father, please help me to trust You enough to release all of my worries and burdens to my Savior Jesus Christ. Help me to no longer carry around the guilt, shame, regret, and all of the other negative emotions that I've carried. Deliver me and rescue me as only You can. I commit my life to You. In Jesus' Name I pray. Amen."

ENCOURAGEMENT OF THE WEEK [#release]

To release baggage and burdens means to let it go, and that's exactly what we must do. Let it all go! Let it go and give it to God! He'll know how to displace and discard it, so that it doesn't re-enter. Give it all to Him and be free, completely free.

SPREAD THE MOTIVATION [#motivate]

Encourage someone to let it go. Let go of all the baggage, emotional trauma, and peace-stealing negative emotions that continue to cause burdens and baggage. Encourage them to give it to God.

Week 26 Motivation

REST IN THE STORM

∞ ∞ ∞

John 16:33 [NIV]

"I have told you these things, so that in Me you may have peace. In this world you will have trouble. But take heart! I have overcome the world."

Dear Friends,

Are you familiar with the popular story about Jesus calming the storm? If not, you've come to the right place for a quick recap of the story. One evening, as Jesus and the disciples were crossing to the other side of the lake, a fierce storm occurred. Keep in mind, it was Jesus' idea to cross to the other side of the lake by boat. The storm was significant enough that it caused the waves to break into the boat, causing the boat to be filled with water. Let's pause for a few seconds and try to imagine how the disciples felt being in a boat that was about to sink because of the combination of thunderous winds and damaging water. They did what any other normal person would have done, they ran to Jesus. Do you remember a time that you were afraid when you were a child? In most cases, that fear led you to run to the person that you knew could comfort and protect you, right?

Well, I'm not exactly sure if that's what the disciples did, but I can tell you that it seemed like they were very afraid and didn't know what to do, so they turned to Jesus, but Jesus was sleeping at the back of the boat with His head on a cushion. Yes, you heard that correctly. Jesus was at the back of the boat sleeping with His head on a cushion, which means He was sleeping peacefully, while the disciples were fearing for their lives in the storm. As they woke Him up shouting for help, He rebuked the wind and silenced the waves, establishing complete peace. Afterwards, He asked the disciples why they were afraid and had no faith. The disciples were terrified and wondered who Jesus truly was because even the wind and the waves obeyed Him. They witnessed firsthand the power of Jesus Christ as He calmed the storm. We can learn a lot from this story, but let's focus on what we should do during a storm.

"IF WE CHOOSE TO PUT OUR COMPLETE TRUST IN THE ONE THAT HAS OVERCOME THE WORLD, THE ONE THAT IS ABLE TO CALM THE STORM, AND THE ONE THAT CAUSES EVERYTHING TO WORK OUT IN OUR FAVOR, WE WILL BE ABLE TO REST IN THE STORM."
[#motivated]

Friends, the disciples were in an actual storm resembling a hurricane, but many of us experience different storms in our lives that have a comparable non-physical impact of a hurricane. Storms are not designed to be easy, simple, or uneventful. They are designed to stretch our faith, increase our trust in God, and cause us to not rely on ourselves, but rely completely on the love and grace of God to sustain us throughout the challenging times. So, what should we do during the storms? The first thing we should do is learn from Jesus. Jesus knew what the outcome would be prior to the occurrence of the storm, which allowed Him to rest very peacefully during the storm. He was not disturbed nor bothered by the storm. He laid His head on a cushion and rested. We should do the same. Grab your cushion and rest. Be at peace and know that Jesus is in the boat with you. You're not alone now and you won't be alone later.

Jesus notified His disciples (us included) that there will be trouble experienced in the world. In other words, there will be challenging times, there will be storms, there will be adverse circumstances, and there will be periods of difficulty that will threaten our lives with hurricane-like impact. He also instructed us to take heart, which means to be at ease and maintain peace, because He has overcome the world. If we choose to put our complete trust in the One that has overcome the world, the One that is able to calm the storm, and the One that causes everything to work out in our favor, we will be able to rest in the storm. It doesn't matter what storm comes our way; we can rest in the peace of Christ. The storm of injustice can't stand against Christ; the storm of persecution can't stand against Christ; the storm of sickness can't stand against Christ; the storm of "not enough" can't stand against Christ; nothing can stand against Jesus Christ. Everything must submit to the authority of Jesus Christ. Everything! That includes us, our problems, and the agents of darkness (demonic forces). If Jesus is an active presence in your life, the authority of Jesus Christ is with you and has enabled you to rest in the storm. Let's choose to maintain the peace of Christ and let it rule in our hearts as we get the most comfortable cushion possible, and rest in the storm.

DEFINE THE PROBLEM | DEVELOP THE SOLUTION

Think about a time that you were very afraid and in a challenging situation. How did you make it out of that situation? It wasn't luck or chance; it was God. God protected you then and He'll protect you now. Trust Him to help you rest in the storm. Here's a quick prayer for you, "Father, please help me to remember that through faith I can make it through any challenging situation. I trust You to give me the endurance and perseverance that I'll need. Please help me to never lack trust, hope, belief, or faith in You and in Your ability to do the impossible. In Jesus' Name I pray. Amen."

ENCOURAGEMENT OF THE WEEK [#assurance]

Assurance in God is full confidence and certainty in His ability to provide and demonstrate His sufficient love for us. We can trust God to do exactly what He always does, and that's extend His unlimited, immeasurable grace to us. It's through God's grace that we're able to rest during the storm, any storm.

SPREAD THE MOTIVATION [#motivate]

Encourage someone to trust God even though it's hard to trust Him during those really difficult situations that we go through.

Week 27 Motivation

BREAK THE CURSE

∞ ∞ ∞

Ezekiel 33:14-16 [NIV]

And if I say to a wicked person, 'You will surely die,' but they then turn away from their sin and do what is just and right—if they give back what they took in pledge for a loan, return what they have stolen, follow the decrees that give life, and do no evil—that person will surely live; they will not die. None of the sins that person has committed will be remembered against them. They have done what is just and right; they will surely live.

Dear Friends,

We're going to start this message with a pop quiz. Based on an earlier message in this book, how would you define a curse? No, not the profanity, swearing, or bad language curse, but the other type of curse. And yes, I'm aware of the new rules that have been developed to have the term "cuss" used as a substitute to define profanity, but I must admit, that word wasn't in my Brooklyn dictionary when I was growing up, so I'm going to treat it like an old bad habit and ignore it [*insert laughter here*]. So, what is a curse? That's a question that's guaranteed to prompt various answers. Some people may immediately think about magic and spells while others may think about bad things happening. Although a curse can be broad in nature, it has the same common endpoint, which is disaster, harm, and destruction. In the previous message, a curse was defined as, "to call upon divine or supernatural power to send injury upon"; "to bring great evil upon"; "evil or misfortune that comes as if in response to imprecation or as retribution"; "to use profanely insolent language against". One of the very first examples of a curse in the Bible comes from Genesis 3:14 in which the serpent was cursed by God for deceiving Eve. The fallout from the disobedience of Adam and Eve was the ground (earth) being cursed. Yes, the entire land was cursed because of man's disobedience (Genesis 3:17). From this we can gather that our actions can bring forth curses. Specifically, actions of disobedience. This is very important to know as we read the Bible because God has never cursed someone for doing what is right. Sure, some people faced different forms of adversity, but the result was never disaster, harm, and destruction.

In the featured scripture, God gave a message to Ezekiel after notifying him that he was being made to be a watchman for the people of Israel. In this message that God gave him, He essentially told the people of Israel that there was a way to break the curse, as He said if a wicked person turns from their sins and does what is just and right, they will live and not die. Although this message was given to a targeted audience, it's very applicable to each of us today. Remember, curses are brought upon through acts of disobedience. Here's something that you may not have known >>> the disobedience of your parents and ancestors can bring forth a curse on you. How? What? Why? In the days of the Bible (Old Testament times), individuals often represented nations. Think about the sons of Noah, the sons of Jacob (also known as Israel), the sons of Esau, and the list goes on and on. When a curse was placed on an individual in those days, it continued throughout bloodlines and generations. Not a single generation, but generations. Need an example? Check out the curse of Canaan (Genesis 9:24-27). Check out Genesis 49:5-7 in which Jacob spoke a curse over Levi's anger and even mentioned that he killed people in anger. Want to know who came from the bloodline of Levi? Moses. Want to know who had moments of anger? Moses. If you recall, Moses even killed an Egyptian (Exodus 2:12). It's important to remember that disobedience left unrepented for spreads and continues to multiply.

"WE'RE ABLE TO CLEANSE THE BLOOD OF DISOBEDIENCE THAT PREVIOUSLY SPREAD THROUGHOUT OUR GENERATIONS BY FILTERING IT WITH THE BLOOD OF JESUS CHRIST."
[#motivated]

Friends, God never intended for the land to be filled with disobedience, but generations grew more and more wicked as they turned away from Him and turned to false gods, idols, and sinful practices. Curses continued to carry on through covenants being knowingly and unknowingly made and renewed with demonic forces/demon gods. What do you think happens when a person chooses to worship a false god? Remember when the Israelites worshipped the golden calf instead of the actual living God that led them out of slavery (Exodus 32)? Don't be too quick to judge and condemn them because people are still worshipping other things today, instead of the actual living God that continues to give us life. Witchcraft and idolatry are no longer being concealed as much today, as we can look around and see the normality of fortune-tellers, "seers", "spiritists", palm-readers, psychics, sorcerers, hypnotists, communicators with the dead, worshippers of ancestors, soul-sellers, and many others that are being tolerated and welcomed. If you don't think anything is wrong with any of that, check out the different events that occurred in the Bible when God's people chose to worship other gods. Curses were always at hand. Today is not any different. Curses continue to spread. It's no coincidence that diseases, health conditions, and self-destructive behavioral commonalities are passed through the blood from generation to generation. This isn't part of God's will for His children. Repentance, redemption, rebirth, and reconciliation is part of God's will for His children.

God made a way for us to break the curse. It's not based on the good deeds or the good words that we communicate at times. It's based on our heart and our individual relationship with the Savior Jesus Christ. It's by God's design that we shall live with Him through His Son Jesus Christ. We break the curse through the redemptive blood of our Lord and Savior Jesus Christ. We're able to cleanse the blood of disobedience that previously spread throughout our generations by filtering it with the blood of Jesus Christ. The blood of Jesus Christ purifies us from all sin (1 John 1:7). The blood of Jesus Christ gives us direct access to the Father (Hebrews 10:19). The blood of Jesus Christ keeps us free from sin (Revelation 1:5). The blood of Jesus Christ isn't physical in nature, but it's given to those that choose to make Jesus Christ their only Lord and Savior. It's the only way to break the curse. Are you ready to break the curse? Start with Jesus Christ and repent for every act of disobedience that you and your ancestors are guilty of and renounce it all, which eliminates the legal access of the demonic forces/demon gods in your life. Submit to God, resist the devil, and he will flee (James 4:7). Break the curse!

DEFINE THE PROBLEM | DEVELOP THE SOLUTION

Are you aware of the curses that are present in your bloodline? If any of your ancestors served other gods, engaged in rebellion or disobedience to God, or dabbled in things that should've been avoided, then more than likely there are curses that were/are prevalent. It's time to break those curses, so that they don't continue to be common in your bloodline. Here's a quick prayer for you, "Father, I humbly submit and surrender myself to You. I reject and renounce all practices of evil in my life. By the blood of my Lord and Savior Jesus Christ, I break and cancel every existing covenant, agreement, partnership, and relationship with sin, evil, darkness, and demonic forces. Let all existing altars and sacrifices be destroyed completely. Let all existing contracts and agreements be null and void. Let all evil flee from me and my bloodline. I do not give any legal right or legal access to any demonic force or demon god. I belong to You Father God and have been washed clean by the blood of my only Lord and Savior Jesus Christ. I submit my entire life to You. In Jesus' Name I pray. Amen."

ENCOURAGEMENT OF THE WEEK [#reject]

Reject all evil, sin, and darkness. Don't give an opening or foothold to demonic forces/demon gods to enter your life. Instead, submit and surrender to God and remain committed to Him for the rest of your life. Allow the blood of the Savior Jesus Christ to cleanse you and cover you completely.

SPREAD THE MOTIVATION [#motivate]

Encourage someone to break the curse by choosing to remain under the covering and protection of the Savior Jesus Christ. This occurs through our continued obedience to Him.

Week 28 Motivation

THE BIGGER THE ATTACK, THE GREATER THE SHIELD

∞ ∞ ∞

2 Kings 6:13-17 [AMP]

So, he said, "Go and see where he is, so that I may send [men] and seize him." And he was told, "He is in Dothan." So, he sent horses and chariots and a powerful army there. They came by night and surrounded the city. The servant of the man of God got up early and went out, and behold, there was an army with horses and chariots encircling the city. Elisha's servant said to him, "Oh no, my master! What are we to do?" Elisha answered, "Do not be afraid, for those who are with us are more than those who are with them." Then Elisha prayed and said, "LORD, please, open his eyes that he may see." And the LORD opened the servant's eyes, and he saw; and behold, the mountain was full of horses and chariots of fire surrounding Elisha.

Dear Friends,

Have you ever been in a very difficult situation that was so troubling it made you question how you would get through that situation? If so, you can somewhat relate to the servant of Elisha in the featured scripture (2 Kings 6). Hopefully, you can't fully relate because that would mean an entire army was coming for you; a very unfriendly army that wasn't there to welcome you to the new neighborhood, but to forcefully remove you from the neighborhood. Let's try to understand the situation that the servant of Elisha experienced. Imagine one day waking up and going out to the porch like you always do, as you check the weather, smell the flowers, sit for a few minutes, and water the lawn, when suddenly you notice a large powerful military unit surrounding your neighborhood and coming for you and the person that you're staying with. Yes, they're coming for you. One of the most normal and logical responses is to be instantly filled with fear.

So, as we reflect on this story, it's understandable that both individuals would be filled with fear. The only problem with that last statement is that there was only one of them that was filled with fear. Remember when I mentioned "normal" and "logical"? Those two terms did not apply to Elisha, who was also referred to as the man of God. He was filled with great faith and assurance. This faith wasn't because he had great physical strength, intellectual power, or a large quantity of weapons. It was completely based on His full confidence in God. He knew that the LORD's army "is" more powerful and mightier than any opposition he could ever face. (Notice that I said "is" more powerful and not "was" more powerful). He knew that God would always protect and shield him from harm.

He confidently and calmly told his servant, "Do not be afraid, for those who are with us are more than those who are with them." Any normal and logical person would have probably said, "I don't see anyone here with us, it's just the two of us", but that's only if we chose to focus on what we saw with our physical eyes, instead of what we continuously see with our eyes of faith. What happened when Elisha asked the LORD to reveal to the servant what Elisha saw all along? "Behold, the mountain was full of horses and chariots of fire surrounding Elisha."

"STAND TOE-TO-TOE AND FACE-TO-FACE WITH YOUR CIRCUMSTANCES AND DECLARE THAT 'I WILL NOT BE AFRAID, FOR HE WHO IS WITH ME IS GREATER THAN THEY THAT ARE AGAINST ME'".
[#motivated]

Friends, it doesn't matter how big or mighty the opposition in your life may seem, if God is for you, there is nothing or no one that can overtake you. Nothing! An army of opposition may surround you, but God's mighty and victorious army is surrounding you as well. Remember this fact >>> the bigger the attack, the greater the shield. Nothing can penetrate God's shield of protection. So, don't allow any of the difficult situations to fill your heart and mind with fear and anxiety. Instead, be reminded that the Creator and Author of life, God, is watching over you. The King of kings and Lord of lords, Jesus Christ, is also watching over you. You are covered! Therefore, stand toe-to-toe and face-to-face with your circumstances and declare that "I will not be afraid, for He who is with me is greater than they that are against me". It doesn't matter what the circumstances are, God is greater! He is our Protector, Healer, Restorer, Redeemer, and Strength. Let's not allow anything to break our faith in Him.

Don't allow the recent attempted attacks on your household, health, finances, relationships, career, ministry, or any other matter of importance in your life convince you to relinquish the irrevocable [permanent, irreversible] peace and joy that you have been granted through Jesus Christ. Put your full complete trust in Him and know that His shield is sufficient for every circumstance. The attacks will not overtake you because God is with you. The challenges cannot break you because God is with you. God is with you! If you've allowed Jesus Christ to enter and remain in your life as your only Lord and Savior, He will always be your Lord and Savior. The bigger the attack, the greater the shield.

DEFINE THE PROBLEM | DEVELOP THE SOLUTION

Think about a time that you were confronted by fear, but you chose to face that fear with the hope that everything would work out. That hope wasn't luck or happenstance, it was God's intervention and protection. He's the armor that we all require in life, so let Him be your armor in all situations that you encounter. Here's a quick prayer for you, "Father, please help me to remain under Your covering, protection, and shield always. Help me to never leave You. You are my refuge and everything that I need in life. Without You, I cannot survive. In Jesus' Name I pray. Amen."

ENCOURAGEMENT OF THE WEEK [#shield]

A shield is meant to protect and equip with defense, providing a sense of comfort and safety. There's no greater shield than God's protection. If He is with You and for You, there's no attack that can overtake you.

SPREAD THE MOTIVATION [#motivate]

Encourage someone to know that God can solve any problem and disarm any threat that attempts to come against us.

Week 29 Motivation
Turn to the Previous Chapter

∞ ∞ ∞

Exodus 16 & 17
(Full Chapters)

Dear Friends,

If I asked you what was going to happen tomorrow, what would your response be? Our answers may vary, but it's possible that the answers will either be based on faith and hope or uncertainty. Life is often filled with the unknown. Yes, uncertainty surrounds us in our daily lives. There's uncertainty of the duration of life (how long will we live?), uncertainty of the exact time of the return of Jesus Christ (when is the last day of the last days?), uncertainty of the challenges that await us (when will we have trouble?), and much more. Our featured scriptures (entire chapters of Exodus 16 & Exodus 17) provide a very good example of uncertainty. As we read chapter 16, we'll notice that the Israelites were traveling through the desert and were uncertain of their next meal, which led to their uncertainty of survival and disbelief of their promised fate. Here's what was said at one point, as they continued to grumble [complain, moan], "If only we had died by the LORD's hand in Egypt! There we sat around pots of meat and ate all the food we wanted, but you have brought us out into this desert to starve this entire assembly to death" (Exodus 16:3, NIV).

Now, let's keep reading and go to chapter 17. In this chapter, we'll notice that the Israelites were filled with uncertainty again, this time it was regarding finding water, which led them to once again doubt the fate that was promised to them, as they grumbled and said, "Why did you bring us up out of Egypt to make us and our children and livestock die of thirst?" (Exodus 17:3, NIV). Unexpected adversity [difficulty, trouble] became a major influence for the uncertainty and doubt that they expressed. God promised that He would deliver them out of Egypt and lead them to a promised land flowing with milk and honey. Their fate was predestined [already determined]. If that was true, why did they continue to let uncertainty control their ability to believe?

"THOSE THAT CHOOSE TO TRUST IN THE LORD SHALL NEVER BE PUT TO SHAME, SHALL NEVER BE FORSAKEN, AND SHALL NEVER BE ABANDONED."

[#motivated]

Friends, much like the Israelites in chapters 16 and 17, we often let uncertainty override our ability to believe and trust God when adversity strikes. So, what exactly happened in each chapter? Well, our first clue would be that they made it past the adversity of chapter 16 because they're in a position to grumble again in chapter 17. In chapter 16, God provided an abundance of food for the people, as Moses told the people, "You will know that it was the LORD when He gives you meat to eat in the evening and all the bread you want in the morning, because He has heard your grumbling against Him. Who are we? You are not grumbling against us, but against the LORD" (Exodus 16:8, NIV). In Chapter 17, God provided the people water, as He told Moses, "I will stand there before you by the rock at Horeb. Strike the rock, and water will come out of it for the people to drink" (Exodus 17:6, NIV). The adversity didn't just stop there, the Israelites were attacked by the Amalekites. Let's pause and think about that. The people grumbled against the LORD for not providing them food and some even disobeyed Him regarding the specific instructions He provided; the people grumbled against the LORD for not providing them water; and now they're getting attacked by distant cousins (FYI, the ancestor of the Israelites is Jacob; the ancestor of the Amalekites is Jacob's twin brother Esau). This was a journey to remember. Surely, they lost this battle, right? Not at all! Check this out:

> "So, Joshua fought the Amalekites as Moses had ordered, and Moses, Aaron and Hur went to the top of the hill. As long as Moses held up his hands, the Israelites were winning, but whenever he lowered his hands, the Amalekites were winning. When Moses' hands grew tired, they took a stone and put it under him, and he sat on it. Aaron and Hur held his hands up—one on one side, one on the other—so that his hands remained steady till sunset. So, Joshua overcame the Amalekite army with the sword" (Exodus 17:10-13, NIV).

There are times in life when we must turn to the previous chapter. Sure, adversity brings forth discomfort, which can cause us to take our eyes off God and forget all that He's done for us, if we allow that to happen. Don't allow that to happen! Don't forget all that God has done for you! God delivered you previously, so you can be certain and believe and trust Him to do it again. He provided the on-time blessing previously, so be certain that He'll do it again. He's the same today as He was yesterday, and when tomorrow occurs, He'll still be the same. The same applies to our Lord and Savior Jesus Christ, as Hebrews 13:8 says, "Jesus Christ is the same yesterday and today and forever (NIV). Our faith reminds us of this fact. Faith gives us a reason to believe, and it assures us of the promises of God in times of uncertainty. Yes, uncertainty may surround us, but faith sustains us. We may not know how the story will be carried out, but we do know how it will end. Those that choose to trust in the LORD shall never be put to shame, shall never be forsaken, and shall never be abandoned. Victory is ours! So, don't let your trials discourage your belief, simply turn to the previous chapter. Yes, turn to the previous chapter! If He did it before, He can do it again.

DEFINE THE PROBLEM | DEVELOP THE SOLUTION

Think about all the times that God intervened in your life when it seemed as if all possibilities were gone and bad things were likely to occur, which will help increase your faith in Him. Here's a quick prayer for you, "Father, help me to always remember the many times that You saved me, delivered me, rescued me, and blessed me. Fill me with the level of faith and trust in You that is pleasing to You. I commit to changing my thoughts, my actions, and my words. In Jesus' Name I pray. Amen."

ENCOURAGEMENT OF THE WEEK [#remember]

Our ability to remember is one of our greatest strengths because it helps us learn from previous experiences. Our ability to remember who God is and what God does is a standard experience for us, and it's vital for our complete faith and trust in Him.

SPREAD THE MOTIVATION [#motivate]

Encourage someone to remember that nothing is impossible for God. It doesn't matter how big the obstacle is, our God is bigger.

Week 30 Motivation
CONTROL WHAT YOU CAN

∞ ∞ ∞

Proverbs 19:21 [NLT]
You can make many plans, but the LORD's purpose will prevail.

Romans 8:28 [NLT]
And we know that God causes everything to work together for the good of those who love God and are called according to His purpose for them.

Dear Friends,

If you had to classify yourself as a planner or non-planner, which one would you be? For further clarity, a planner in this scenario would be the person that likes to (or must) plan their daily activities and generally does not like when their plans are off schedule. The non-planner in this scenario would be the person that doesn't like to or rarely plans their daily activities and generally prefers to react to situations as they occur. Here's a follow-up question, what do you do when things happen that are not within your control? Before you answer that question, let's look at the featured scripture that notifies us that we can "make many plans, but the LORD's purpose will prevail". That's the polite way of saying, "It really doesn't matter what you want to do if your plans don't align with God's purpose". Sounds harsher than it is. In fact, it's a protection and a blessing for us. How many times have you wanted something or wanted to do something that would've been very bad for you in the long run, but it was blocked from getting to you? FYI, I'm not talking about eating that extra dessert that would've put you over your daily calorie intake limit or us remembering the days of our youth and attempting to resurrect that old hairstyle we once had that should've remained in the past [*insert laughter here*].

The point is that things get prevented because God causes everything to work together for the good of those who love Him and are called according to His purpose for them. We must accept the fact that some things are out of our control, which can be good and not so good at times. We can't control how long we'll live on earth; we can't control who will like or dislike us; we can't control how other people behave or react; we can't control how and when God chooses to answer our prayers; we can't control some of the adverse occurrences and circumstances in our lives; and the list goes on and on. However, we can control what we can control. What can we control?

"WE CAN CONTROL HOW WE RESPOND TO LIFE AND HOW WE RESPOND IN LIFE."
[#motivated]

Friends, take a few seconds to think about some of the things that you can control [*insert a 20-second pause here*]. I'm sure that you were able to come up with several things, but for the purposes of this message, let's focus on the most significant. We can control how we respond to life and how we respond in life. This covers a lot because it's a broad statement, so let's go a bit deeper. We can control our level of faith, correct? Faith is a choice, as is hope, belief, and trust. We can control how much faith, hope, belief, and trust we choose to place in God daily, especially when we're faced with challenges and adverse occurrences that aren't within our control. We can also control how we choose to respond to potential conflict, disagreements, differences, and difficult situations. We can choose to have self-control and respond thoughtfully and gracefully (as we remember the good advice noted in Ephesians 4:26 that says, in your anger do not sin), or we can choose to allow our emotions to control us, which will generally result in more harm than good. Like the first point, we can choose who and/or what we listen to and accept as truth. This is very important.

Do you know that the devil attempted to tempt Jesus and deceive Him with modified truth like how the serpent used modified truth to trick Eve in the Garden? For quick reference, check out Matthew 4 and Genesis 3. Jesus chose to listen to God and the complete truth that is His word. He chose to submit to God, resist the devil, and as a result the devil had to flee from Him. Jesus provided us the blueprint of how to respond to/in life. It's no coincidence that James 4:7 says, "Submit yourselves, then, to God. Resist the devil, and he will flee from you" (NIV). Control what you can control! Choose to be humble instead of prideful. Choose to be obedient to God instead of obedient to the devil. Choose to walk in love instead of hate. Choose to forgive instead of holding on to baggage of unforgiveness. Choose to maintain peace instead of stress, chaos, and dysfunction. Choose Jesus Christ, He's the Way, the Truth, and the Life. Control how you respond to everything that happens in life, and trust God to control everything else – all of life's intricate [complex, complicated] details. He'll work it all out for your good, as you keep loving Him. Control what you can!

DEFINE THE PROBLEM | DEVELOP THE SOLUTION

Think about a time that things did not work out as you planned, but ended up working out exactly the way that you hoped for. It wasn't a coincidence, nor was it chance or luck. It was God. God saw your plans, but had His perfect plan for your situation. Remember that and hold on to the fact that we can't control everything. Here's a quick prayer for you, "Father, please help me to relinquish my desire to control everything. Help me to fully trust You, which means letting go and trusting that You know what's best and trusting Your timing for everything. In Jesus' Name I pray. Amen."

Encouragement of the Week [#control]

The greatest form of control is self-control. Why? Because it's the only type of control that we truly always have, if we choose to. It's a gift and ability given to us by God.

Spread the Motivation [#motivate]

Encourage someone to know that it's okay if a situation doesn't go as planned, but goes according to God's plan. Show them how to trust God and trust that He knows best.

Week 31 Motivation
DON'T LIMIT GOD

∞ ∞ ∞

Luke 7:11-15 [NLT]

Soon afterward Jesus went with His disciples to the village of Nain, and a large crowd followed Him. A funeral procession was coming out as He approached the village gate. The young man who had died was a widow's only son, and a large crowd from the village was with her. When the Lord saw her, His heart overflowed with compassion. "Don't cry!" He said. Then He walked over to the coffin and touched it, and the bearers stopped. "Young man," He said, "I tell you, get up." Then the dead boy sat up and began to talk! And Jesus gave him back to his mother.

(Also read Luke 8:40-56)

Dear Friends,

What's your most interesting encounter with God? If you say you haven't had any and are reading or listening to this message, you've had some type of interaction with Him. Why else would you listen to or read about a message about God? For many of us, our favorite encounters would probably involve God performing some type of miracle in our lives or doing something that only He could do. Guess what? He's been doing that since the beginning of creation because that's what He does and it's who He is. He's omnipotent [unlimited power], omniscient [unlimited knowledge], and omnipresent [present everywhere at the same time]. He's God! What if I told you that even though we know all of these things about God, many of us still choose to place restrictions on His ability, would you believe me? Unfortunately, that's a true statement and it's because of our limited or conditional faith. FYI, conditional means it's based on some type of condition, stipulation, or circumstance. Thus, conditional faith means a type of faith that isn't absolute, but is based on conditions. If the conditions are met, then we will believe. In other words, it's limited.

Do you think our God wants us to have temporary trust in Him? Of course not! This means that conditional faith can't be God-approved. If something isn't God-approved, it can't be pleasing to Him. Here's a very important life tip >>> when there's a choice to be made between pleasing God and pleasing people, you should always choose the One that's omnipotent, omniscient, and omnipresent. Yes, that would be God. Hebrews 13:5, which is based on Deuteronomy 31:6, reminds us that God previously said to His people that He will never leave them nor forsake them. Although this was said to His people long ago in Israel, it's still applicable to His people today. His people are those that have accepted His Son Jesus Christ as their only Lord and Savior. The reason why Hebrews 13:5 was mentioned is because it's an important reminder for us that God's promises are true, even when we're confronted by great odds, adverse circumstances, or challenging times. He'll never leave us nor forsake us.

"THERE IS NO TASK TOO DIFFICULT, NO PROBLEM TOO COMPLICATED, NO THREAT TOO DANGEROUS, NOR NO OPPOSITION TOO POWERFUL FOR OUR GOD."
[#motivated]

Friends, what if you would've witnessed Jesus raise the widow's son in Luke 7? Would you have unconditional faith after seeing that? Would that have caused you to possess a level of faith as Jairus and the woman who had been subject to bleeding for twelve years in Luke 8? Why did I mention those two? Because they chose to not limit God's ability as they displayed the faith in Jesus Christ that God desires His children to have. Not limiting God and truly believing in His unlimited ability is an important component of faith, which is why we're reminded in Luke 18:27 that "What is impossible with man is possible with God" (NIV). Yes, what is impossible with man is possible with God. This was said to remind us of God's unlimited ability, which surpasses our understanding. If we choose to put our complete trust in Him and believe that He can do the impossible, we can guarantee that everything will work out in our favor, according to His perfect plan and purpose. Yes, He's omnipotent, omniscient, and omnipresent, but most of all He is our Father that loves us unconditionally and the One that will never leave us nor forsake us. He didn't leave Jairus who threw himself at the feet of Jesus to save his daughter's life. He didn't forsake the woman who believed that Jesus was the cure to her twelve-year battle with continuous bleeding.

Is there a situation that you're going through that seems too impossible to resolve? Remember the widow's son in the featured scripture. Jesus restored his life after he was already dead. If God can allow life to be restored into a dead person, He can resolve the situation in your life through our Lord and Savior Jesus Christ. Trust Him and believe in His ability! There is no task too difficult, no problem too complicated, no threat too dangerous, nor no opposition too powerful for our God. He can and will do the impossible, if we trust and believe in Him. Let's choose to have an increased level of unconditional faith as we choose to not place restrictions on God's ability. Don't limit God!

DEFINE THE PROBLEM | DEVELOP THE SOLUTION

Think about a time that you witnessed a miracle. It may not have been a miracle in the eyes of others, but you knew that there was only one way that the situation could've happened like it did. It was God! That was God reminding you that He can do it. Continue to trust Him to meet your needs, all of your needs. If He did it before, you can trust and believe wholeheartedly that your Father can do it again. Here's a quick prayer for you, "Father, please help me to remove all doubt. Let me not entertain anything that goes against my unconditional belief and trust in You. Help me to place no limitations on Your ability to do the impossible. It may be impossible for us human beings, but nothing is impossible for You. Help me to never have conditional faith. In Jesus' Name I pray. Amen."

ENCOURAGEMENT OF THE WEEK [#reassurance]

Nothing is impossible for God. He sees everything, knows everything, hears everything, and can do anything. He's also in full control of everything and must give consent before anything occurs. He's also our Father. A Father that loves His children who are covered by His Son Jesus Christ's blood. Be reassured that our God, our Father, and our Savior can do anything.

SPREAD THE MOTIVATION [#motivate]

Encourage someone to trust God, even when it's hard to maintain faith. He knows everything and can do anything, so let that be the reassuring comfort that's needed.

Week 32 Motivation

FOLLOW HIS LEAD

∞ ∞ ∞

Philippians 2:3-5 [NLT]
Don't be selfish; don't try to impress others. Be humble, thinking of others as better than yourselves. Don't look out only for your own interests, but take an interest in others, too. You must have the same attitude that Christ Jesus had.

Dear Friends,

This may be a shocking surprise, but did you know that the world we live in is filled with a lot of selfishness? Okay, maybe you were already fully aware of that, so let's add more context. In addition to selfishness, we'll also notice that the world is filled with pride, arrogance, egoism, conceit, and a lack of genuine concern for others. All of which are the exact opposite of what Jesus demonstrated during His life on earth. The featured scripture notifies us that we must have the same attitude that Jesus had. If we continue reading through the chapter, we'll gain a better understanding of the correct attitude to have, as it says, "Though He was God, He did not think of equality with God as something to cling to. Instead, He gave up His divine privileges; He took the humble position of a slave and was born as a human being. When He appeared in human form, He humbled Himself in obedience to God and died a criminal's death on a cross" (Philippians 2:6-8, NLT). Think about that for a moment. Jesus gave up His divine privileges and humbled Himself.

If we're being completely honest with ourselves, it's difficult for a lot of us to be humble when we gain a high position, power, authority, or increased wealth. It's a major reality check because none of our "big" accomplishments compare to what Jesus selflessly gave up for the purpose of being completely obedient to God. Jesus showed us how to trust and obey God, even when it may not make sense to the world. For instance, does it make sense for the wealthiest King on earth to live as a mere carpenter's son? Does it make sense for the wisest Man on earth to submit to other human beings? Does it make sense for the most powerful Man on earth to allow Himself to be persecuted on a cross when He could've easily stopped the entire thing? I think I can answer for most of us and say "no", it doesn't make sense in the world that we live in, which makes it that much more meaningful when we follow His lead.

"SOMETIMES IN LIFE, WE MUST TUNE OUT THE OUTSIDE NOISE AND MUTE ALL OF THE DISTRACTIONS. THIS IS THE ONLY WAY THAT WE'LL PREVENT THE GUILT-TRAPS, BAIT-GRABS, AND GROWTH-STOPPERS."
[#motivated]

Friends, following His lead may not make sense to others, but it will make sense to your spirit. That's all that matters. Your spirit craves God and everything that He provides. To live without God is equivalent to depriving the spirit of its essential nutrients. Sometimes in life, we must tune out the outside noise and mute all of the distractions. This is the only way that we'll prevent the "guilt-traps", "bait-grabbers", and "growth-stoppers". Yes, I just made those terms up, but they fit the message very well, so feel free to use them in your next message that you share with others who need Jesus Christ. Back to the message. To achieve what God has reserved for us, we're going to have to follow Jesus' approach and humble ourselves. This means it doesn't matter how much authority we have over others, how much wealth we have, or how much knowledge and credentials we have. None of it matters to God because He's the Creator of life and He's the Giver of all great gifts. Do you understand that? Everything that you have may seem like it's because of your hard work and dedication, but guess Who allowed things to work out for you? Guess Who allowed you to wake up and breathe? Guess Who didn't allow sin to end your life? God!

One of the few things that God asks of us is to be humble and give Him the glory. Is that too difficult? For some it is, but hopefully this helps. After Jesus completely humbled Himself and fully obeyed God, notice what happened, as Philippians 2:9-11 says, "Therefore, God elevated Him to the place of highest honor and gave Him the Name above all other names, that at the Name of Jesus every knee should bow, in heaven and on earth and under the earth, and every tongue declare that Jesus Christ is Lord, to the glory of God the Father" (NLT). Because of His obedience to God, Jesus returned to His divine privileges and is elevated to the place of highest honor. Highest honor! There's no name greater than the Name of Jesus Christ. I know He's referred to as different names in different languages, but no matter what He's called in our different languages, He's still the only Christ, the Savior, the Messiah, the Redeemer, and the Risen King.

None of us have a valid excuse to not be humble. Whatever it is that we have, Jesus had more and still maintained a humble heart. Pride isn't a good thing. If you're holding on to pride (knowingly or unknowingly), it's time to let it go. According to Jesus, "Those who exalt themselves will be humbled, and those who humble themselves will be exalted" (Matthew 23:11, NLT). Keep this in mind when you're tempted to boast about what you have, what you've done, or what you know. Keep this in mind when you're tempted to prolong [extend, lengthen] the argument because your pride won't let you walk away. Keep this in mind when your pride won't allow you to admit that you're wrong or accept corrections. Keep this in mind when your pride won't allow you to submit to God. Pride is not worth the complications [problems, difficulties] that it causes. It causes many problems that should be avoided. Let's follow Jesus' lead and humble ourselves. Guess what happens next? The blessings await the humble.

DEFINE THE PROBLEM | DEVELOP THE SOLUTION

Think about a time that you accomplished something big, something major that made you feel extremely successful. How did you do it? How did you celebrate? If God wasn't included in your responses, that means pride lurked somewhere in the mix. Excluding God is equivalent to removing God. Learn from the previous mistakes and choose to be completely humble, recognizing and acknowledging that God is the reason for the victory. Here's a quick prayer for you, "Father, please help me to always remain humble. No matter how much success I have on earth, help me to remember that You make it all possible. Your love, grace, and mercy are the reasons that I'm able to do what I do and have what I have. Help me to give You all the glory possible. In Jesus' Name I pray. Amen."

ENCOURAGEMENT OF THE WEEK [#humble]

Being humble is one of the greatest skills and abilities that a person could have. It's also one of the most rewarding and admirable characteristic traits as well. Not only does it attract blessings, but it also causes us to be recognized by God. Is it more important to be recognized by other people or by God? No contest! God exalts the humble, so be humble and know that God is the Provider of everything good. His glory, His praise, His credit, His worship!

SPREAD THE MOTIVATION [#motivate]

Encourage someone to choose to be humble instead of prideful, proud, and arrogant. Remind them that it's much better to humble ourselves voluntarily than to have God humble us involuntarily.

Week 33 Motivation
GOD HAS THE FINAL SAY

∞ ∞ ∞

Proverbs 16:1 [GNT]
We may make our plans, but God has the last word.

Dear Friends,

Have you ever quit or gave up on something because it was too difficult? If so, how did you feel afterwards? Notice, I said something that was "too difficult", which excludes the time you quit that job because your manager didn't appreciate you and your excellent work, and quitting was a way of maintaining your peace. I'm talking about walking away from something that would've benefitted you had you stuck around long enough to get through it. Yes, the very difficult, very challenging, very tough, yet very rewarding things. Let's add to our initial question. Have you ever quit or gave up on something because it was too difficult, but you ended up having to do it anyway? If so, that's a big reminder that "we may make our plans, but God has the last word". God has the final say in the matter. If He wants us to experience different faith-building, level-increasing, growth-prompting adversity, that's exactly what will happen. Keep in mind, adversity can be in the form of negative situations, unfortunate circumstances, storms, trials, challenges, tests, and unforeseen events that appear to cause harm.

Throughout the course of life, each of us will experience some form of adversity at some point in time. Some experiences will be more extreme than others, but the response must be the same. We must trust that God has the final say. Trusting God requires complete faith during all circumstances, whether good or bad. Unfortunately, we're not able to select the tests and trials that we want to go through, however, we are able to determine our response. What will your response be?

"IT DOESN'T MATTER WHAT CIRCUMSTANCES CONFRONT US, GOD'S LOVE FOR US IS FAR GREATER."
[#motivated]

Friends, many of us have already made plans to give up because the challenges are too difficult (e.g., relationship with God, marriage, parenthood, financial management, health, etc.). Giving up is often considered the easy way out, but its consequences are far more significant than we may think. Can you imagine if Jesus would've given up because the thought of bearing all of our sins on the cross was too difficult to accept? Or what if

God would've given up on mankind after the disobedience of Adam and Eve? The result would not have been good, correct? In fact, none of us would be where we are today if God had given up on us and if Jesus had not given His life on the cross in exchange for ours. We must return the favor and not give up on God because the challenges seem too difficult for us to get through. Keep in mind, when we choose to quit or give up, we display a level of distrust in God. We choose escape, safety, and fear over faith, trust, and purpose. With God, there's always a positive in every negative. Usually, the positive is found in His unlimited love and sufficient grace, which ultimately results in perseverance being fully displayed in our lives. The more we trust God, the more we persevere.

Trusting God should never be optional. It should be our conditioned response to every form of adversity that we face in life. It doesn't matter what circumstances confront us, God's love for us is far greater. We will always have victory through Jesus Christ. Jesus is our Savior, Redeemer, Deliverer, and Source for life. There's nothing too difficult for Him to overcome, and He has given us His Holy Spirit, which means there's nothing too difficult for us to overcome if we maintain our trust in Him. Let's remember that God has the final say.

DEFINE THE PROBLEM | DEVELOP THE SOLUTION

Think about a time that you were about to quit or give up because the challenges seemed impossible to overcome, but you ended up sticking it out and working through it. How did you feel afterwards? Endurance and perseverance were given to you, not by coincidence, but by God. Remember that the next time you're tempted to take the easy way out by giving up. Here's a quick prayer for you, "Father, please help me to not give in to temptation and choose to give up when adversity arises. Help me to remain committed to You, knowing that You are in full control and will always have the final say. Help my trust in You to not be conditional or limited. Help me to trust You always, no matter the circumstance. In Jesus' Name I pray. Amen."

ENCOURAGEMENT OF THE WEEK [#resilience]

Resilience is given to those that choose to put their complete trust in God. Resilience helps us get through times of difficulties, not quit during difficult tests and trials, and keep pushing with faith. If we desire to be resilient in life, we must never give up on God.

SPREAD THE MOTIVATION [#motivate]

Encourage someone to keep pushing through the challenges of life by trusting in God and not giving up. Let them know that there's a positive in every negative with God.

Week 34 Motivation

DISCERNING DISTRACTIONS

∞ ∞ ∞

Matthew 4:5-7 [GNT]

Then the Devil took Jesus to Jerusalem, the Holy City, set Him on the highest point of the Temple, and said to Him, "If you are God's Son, throw Yourself down, for the scripture says, 'God will give orders to His angels about You; they will hold You up with their hands, so that not even Your feet will be hurt on the stones.'" Jesus answered, "But the scripture also says, 'Do not put the LORD your God to the test.'"

Dear Friends,

Have you ever tried to work on something important, but kept getting interrupted by something or someone? No, I'm not talking about something "very important" like watching a TV show or eating a big bowl of ice cream that we probably shouldn't have had anyway, I'm talking about something more important in life, maybe something along the lines of studying for the big exam, updating the budget and expenses, finishing a big assignment, reading this excellent book that you're reading now, or even better, reading the greatest book of all time, the Bible, and using the scriptures to help you pray. If you have been interrupted, think about how you felt at the time. Interruptions are usually unpleasant, unless it's an interruption that feeds our wants and desires. When this happens, the wants and desires could become distractions.

Consider the featured scripture in which Jesus encountered a distraction. If you're not familiar with this story, this is the passage about Jesus being led into the wilderness by the Spirit, and after fasting for forty days and forty nights, He was going to be tempted by the devil on three separate occasions. The featured scripture picks up at the second occasion, where the devil quoted the Word of God (he quoted Psalm 91:11-12), but Jesus discerned and recognized the distraction and counteracted it with God's truth (the perfect countermeasure via Deuteronomy 6:16). What was the distraction? The distraction was the Word of God being used in an intentional incorrect manner for purposes of manipulation and deception. Remember, our wants and desires can become distractions. It wasn't difficult to see that Jesus always desired the Word of God (remember, He is the Word of God in the flesh), but the Word of God that was being inappropriately used by the devil in a plot to mislead, trick, and deceive Him became a distraction that Jesus rejected immediately. He chose to focus on the mission and not the temptation [lure, attraction]. What can we learn from this?

"God will never abandon us to temptation, manipulation, or deception. He'll give us the help we need to overcome everything, but we must accept His help."
[#motivation]

Friends, there are three things that we can learn from the excellent response of Jesus. First, it's very important for each of us to know what the Word of God says for ourselves. If we must rely on others to tell us what it says, it's highly likely that we'll be deceived at some point because of the message being taken out of context, inadvertently or purposely. Second, it's very important for each of us to discern [detect, recognize] distractions. Distractions often appear when we're attempting to grow or change for the better. Distractions usually appeal to the desires of the flesh and become roadblocks in our lives. This means that we start wanting the things (or people) that we should stay far, far away from. God gives us discernment, which allows us to recognize the distractions and see their true intent and motives, as well as an immediate glimpse of the negative consequences. Third, it's very important for each of us to know what our God-assigned mission is, which will help us tune out the noise that comes from distractions. When we know what God is calling us to do, anything that attempts to contradict those things becomes a distraction that's equivalent to a bunch of noise. What do we do with a bunch of noise? Tune it out!

Discerning distractions is not an easy task, primarily because distractions are generally things that interest us, but God! It's important to remember that God will never abandon us to temptation, manipulation, or deception. He'll give us the help we need to overcome everything, but we must accept His help. Jesus didn't fall for the tricks of the devil. Each time, He responded with the truth. Look at what happened in the end, after all of the failed attempts by the devil were complete, as the scripture says, "Then the Devil left Jesus; and angels came and helped Him" (Matthew 4:11, NIV). When we reject the distractions, the distractions will leave. Say that again, again, and again. When you, when I, when we reject the distractions, the distractions will leave. It's time to start rejecting. Discern the distractions and reject them completely and immediately, just like Jesus did. Let's focus on the mission and trust God to lead the way.

Define the Problem | Develop the Solution

Think about the distractions in your life and the reasons why they are distractions. What are those distractions trying to prevent you from achieving or accomplishing? Don't accept those distractions and allow them to have power over you. Instead, discern and reject. Understand when it's time to move on and leave stuff behind. Here's a quick prayer for you, "Father, please help me to discern distractions and everything in my life that is hindering me from growing and maturing in Jesus Christ. Help me to never lose sight of the mission and the calling that You have given me. Help me to honor You completely. In Jesus' Name I pray. Amen."

ENCOURAGEMENT OF THE WEEK [#discern]

God gives us the ability to discern distractions and the authority to reject distractions. There's no need to continue to entertain distractions. Discern and reject! Recognize the distractions, understand what the distractions are attempting to prevent and accomplish, and rid yourself of the distractions. Use the power and ability that God has given you.

SPREAD THE MOTIVATION [#motivate]

Encourage someone to get rid of all distractions, no matter who or what they are, as they make a choice to live completely and wholeheartedly for God.

Week 35 Motivation
GROWN UP & SAVED

∞ ∞ ∞

1 Peter 2:1-2 [GNT]
Rid yourselves, then, of all evil; no more lying or hypocrisy or jealousy or insulting language. Be like newborn babies, always thirsty for the pure spiritual milk, so that by drinking it you may grow up and be saved.

Dear Friends,

How many times have you heard someone say, "it's time to grow up!"? Or maybe I should've asked, how many times have you told someone that "it's time to grow up!"? It's a phrase that parents are very familiar with, even when the phrase doesn't truly apply to the situation at hand. For example, when your child has a messy room with papers from six years ago overflowing, we may say, "it's time to grow up!"; when your child refuses to take daily vitamins and then gets sick and spreads the germs to the rest of the household, we may say, "it's time to grow up!"; when your child can't seem to remember to empty the lunchbox every day, but can somehow remember that you promised frozen yogurt eighteen weeks ago, we may say, "it's time to grow up!" [*insert laughter here*]. The point is, it's a common phrase that's often spoken when a level of immaturity is present. Throughout the course of life, we're all expected to reach certain milestones in our growth and development cycle. Think about it! We go through the infant phase, then toddler phase, then elementary phase, then adolescent phase, then young adulthood phase, then adulthood phase, and then the beloved senior phase. During each phase, we're expected to grow and develop because of time and experiences. Generally, more wisdom, knowledge, understanding, and discernment is gained as we increase in age. Notice I said "generally", which means it's not always the case. I'm sure we can start going down the list of adult family members that missed the memo and have been in our "Father, please help them" prayer requests for the past several years, but we're still going to keep hoping and believing for the miracle of maturity to take place, right?

What if I told you that there are spiritual growth and development phases as well? Would that cause you to assess your life and the decisions that you make more carefully? It's true! We go through spiritual growth and development phases, just like we go through physical growth and development cycles. Although it would be great to correlate [connect, link] age with spiritual maturity, it doesn't always work that way. Have you ever seen or met an adult that had no knowledge of how to live for God? I'm almost certain that we all have. If you're someone that doesn't know how to live for God, don't feel ashamed, it's not too late to make a life-altering, life-saving decision to live for God through the acceptance of Jesus Christ. We all have room to grow, which means we all must grow up and be saved. What exactly does that mean?

> *"WE MAY HAVE BEEN BORN INTO SIN WITH A BLOODLINE FILLED WITH DETESTABLE EVILS, BUT JESUS CHRIST GIVES US THE ABILITY TO BE BORN AGAIN."*
> *[#motivated]*

Friends, we can assess our level of maturity by the presence or existence of evil in our lives. If our actions are indicative [telling, revealing] of the evil that's in our heart and mind, then that's a clear indicator that we still have a lot of growing up to do. In other words, the presence or existence of evil in our lives equals immaturity. Lying, hypocrisy, jealousy, and insulting language are just a handful of common evil practices. To grow up, we must rid ourselves of all of those things. Need more examples? Throw in idolatry, witchcraft, sexual immorality, pride, rebellion, dishonesty, deception, lust, drunkenness, greed, selfishness, and the list of evil behavior goes on and on. These are all things that we may have been born into or things that may be prevalent in our bloodlines. This is where the saved part becomes relevant. To be saved means to be delivered, rescued, and set free. We were delivered, rescued, and set free from the power of sin when Jesus Christ died on the cross and was resurrected three days later. Yes, we may have been born into sin with a bloodline filled with detestable evils, but Jesus Christ gives us the ability to be born again. Jesus Christ gives us the ability to have a new identity with His perfect blood flowing through our spiritual bodies. Jesus Christ gives us the ability to be grown up and saved amid the evil that fills the world. Yes, it is Jesus Christ, the Son of God, that helps us get rid of all the immature acts of evil and leads us through the spiritual growth and development stages that we ought to go through. In other words, the active presence and existence of Jesus Christ in our lives equals maturity.

So, what are we to do now? Always thirst for pure spiritual milk. No matter how old or young you are, always thirst for pure spiritual milk that comes directly from our Savior Jesus Christ. The students (us) will never outgrow the Teacher (Jesus), so we'll always have room to learn and grow. Add to your wisdom, knowledge, understanding, and discernment. Consider 1 Corinthians 13:11, which says, "When I was a child, I talked like a child, I thought like a child, I reasoned like a child. When I became a man, I put the ways of childhood behind me" (NIV). Let's no longer think and behave like immature children. Let's rid ourselves of evil, so that we may truly grow up. Let's start the saved cycle by giving Jesus Christ complete access and oversight of our entire lives. Withhold nothing from Him. Let's be grown up and saved!

DEFINE THE PROBLEM | DEVELOP THE SOLUTION

Think about a period in your life when you were immature or lacked knowledge and awareness. Did your immaturity help or hurt you? Unless a lesson was learned, it probably didn't help you, but it's not too late to learn. Learn from those experiences to help you make better decisions moving forward. Knowledge and awareness are bundled with God's grace and love for us. Remember that as you continue to grow and develop. Here's a quick prayer for you, "Father, please help me to never stop learning from Your teaching. Help me to be teachable and open to Your correction, guidance, and direction. Help me to glorify You with my whole heart and allow my actions to reflect my love for You. In Jesus' Name I pray. Amen."

ENCOURAGEMENT OF THE WEEK [#develop]

Our spiritual growth and development are completely reliant and dependent on our intimate relationship with God and the Savior Jesus Christ. For us to mature, we must first have the relationship with God. He's our Father and Source for life, so it's important for us to include Him in our daily lives.

SPREAD THE MOTIVATION [#motivate]

Encourage someone to not exclude God, but include God in their daily lives. Including the greatest Counselor and Teacher in our lives will help improve our decision-making, which will lead to good and wise decisions being made.

Week 36 Motivation

KEEP ON!

∞ ∞ ∞

Matthew 7:7-8 [NLT]

Keep on asking, and you will receive what you ask for. Keep on seeking, and you will find. Keep on knocking, and the door will be opened to you. For everyone who asks, receives. Everyone who seeks, finds. And to everyone who knocks, the door will be opened.

Dear Friends,

Have you ever really wanted something, but didn't get it? Most likely, we all can answer this question with a big "yes", and that's because throughout the course of life we do not always get everything that we want. Yes, it's an unfortunate truth, but it's the truth, nonetheless. It doesn't matter how much money or wealth we have; it doesn't matter how clever and resourceful we are; it doesn't matter who or what we know; it doesn't matter what status we have; it just doesn't matter. We can't get what we want all the time. If you're thinking that money and power can get us everything that we want, think again. Money and power can't buy the peace of Christ. Need proof? Check out what happened to Pharaoh (read Exodus 12), King Saul (read 1 Samuel 18), Naaman (read 2 Kings 5), and even Solomon (read the book of Ecclesiastes). All of them learned the valuable life lesson that no amount of money and power will ever be enough to buy peace. That's a fulfillment that can only be fulfilled by God via Jesus Christ. So, know that the sustainable peace that we all desire can only come from God via Jesus. Without Jesus there's no sustainable peace. Temporary peace may be possible, but it doesn't last. The true peace that lasts all seasons, perseveres through all occurrences, and remains intact throughout the course of life is provided by God via Jesus. Remember that!

Now, let's get back to the message. There are a few common tendencies that are shared by people when we don't get what we want. I'm not going to include tantrums [outbursts, fits], since we're all past that type of behavior, but many of us tend to rebel when we don't get what we want (which is a type of tantrum). Rebellion causes self-damage and curses, so that's clearly not worth it. Some of us allow our emotions to guide our actions, as anger, sadness, envy, jealousy, and the rest of the "peace-stealers" lead us through the doom and gloom paths that we ought to stay away from. Some people choose to keep pursuing, but pursuing something that belongs to someone else or is intended for someone else can cause serious problems.

How about we turn to God for the correct response?!? According to the featured scripture, there's a standard response that we all should take, and that's to keep on!

"When we choose to put our complete trust, hope, faith, and belief in God, He moves on our behalf."
[#motivate]

Friends, if you're going to God and are asking for something specific and you don't get it the first time around, don't quit or give up because it's taking longer than you expected. Keep on! (Asking, seeking, and knocking). Notice, I said going to God. Putting God first, above all of our selfish and greedy desires, and trusting Him is the prerequisite [requirement, condition] to any ask of God. When God is first, it doesn't matter what the ask is. Understand and know that God can provide. He is well-pleased by pure hearts, pure motives, and pure lives that rely and depend completely on Him (demonstration of faith and trust). Do you know what that means? That means that nothing is impossible for God, and nothing is impossible for us when we choose to put our faith in God (read Mark 9:23). In other words, when we choose to put our complete trust, hope, faith, and belief in God, He moves on our behalf. What's the result? The result is answered prayers, unexpected blessings, and unimaginable growth. Not to be misleading, there are times when we don't get what we ask for, and that's simply because God knows best. He'll never purposely lead us into destruction, which is why some of the things that we ask for aren't granted. In other words, the things that we ask for may not be in our best interest to receive. However, we won't know unless we ask, right?

So, today, if you have yet to receive an answer from God, and you're still in need, you must keep on. If it's healing in your body and/or mind that you want, keep on! If it's peace that you want in your life and household, keep on! If it's relief from storms and challenges that you want, keep on! If it's salvation and deliverance that you want for your loved ones that are lost, keep on! Whatever it is, keep on! Don't stop! Keep on asking until you receive what you're asking for or get an answer from God. Keep on seeking until you find what you're looking for. Keep on knocking until God opens the door. This is what He wants us to do, so let's do it. Let's be relentless in prayer, let's be persistent in faith, and let's be prepared to receive. Keep on!

DEFINE THE PROBLEM | DEVELOP THE SOLUTION

Think about a time that you asked God for something and didn't get what you asked for immediately. How did that make you feel? Were you motivated to keep asking or were you tempted to give up? Whatever the situation was, use that experience to help you move forward. Keep asking God and keep trusting Him, no matter how long it takes. Here's a quick prayer for you, "Father, please help me to never stop trusting You and trusting Your timing. You have a reason for me not getting what I ask for when I ask for it, and I thank You for creating in me patience and persistent hope. Help me to always know that You have a perfect plan for me and all of my brothers and sisters. In Jesus' Name I pray. Amen."

ENCOURAGEMENT OF THE WEEK [#persistence]

Persistence is motivation to keep on. When we are persistent in prayer, hope, faith, and trust in God, we establish a continued belief of expectation based on God's ability to provide what we need and what He wants us to have. It's the ultimate assurance based on faith.

SPREAD THE MOTIVATION [#motivate]

Encourage someone to be persistent in faith and prayer, as they trust God to be the Provider and Deliverer that He is. He knows what we need and when we need it.

Week 37 Motivation
HE IS FOR YOU

∞ ∞ ∞

Romans 8:31 [GNT]
In view of all this, what can we say? If God is for us, who can be against us?

Romans 8:38-39 [NLT]
And I am convinced that nothing can ever separate us from God's love. Neither death nor life, neither angels nor demons, neither our fears for today nor our worries about tomorrow—not even the powers of hell can separate us from God's love. No power in the sky above or in the earth below—indeed, nothing in all creation will ever be able to separate us from the love of God that is revealed in Christ Jesus our Lord.

Dear Friends,

Have you ever felt as if you were all alone even though you weren't? Have you ever felt abandoned by God even though you weren't? Have you ever felt lost and hopeless even though you weren't? These are all fair questions for us to consider. If we're completely honest with ourselves, many of us have felt all of the above at some point in our lives. Not to be ashamed, sometimes we experience ups and downs throughout the course of life, which leads us to believe false truths and narratives about ourselves and our situations. We accept these lies and deception because they make sense to our human minds. The false truths will tell us that the storms and challenges we're experiencing are solely because of the sin in our lives. It won't let us know that sometimes we must experience adversity and faith-increasing challenges to grow in the faith that we have in Jesus Christ. The false truths will try to convince us that sin has separated us from God so much that there's no possible way we could ever go back to Him. It won't let us know that nothing can separate us from God's love that is revealed in Christ Jesus, and the road of repentance is our path to Jesus. The false truths will also tell us that it's okay to worry and be afraid about the things we cannot control because we're human. It'll neglect to mention that God did not give us a spirit of fear, and fear that is continued is the opposite of what God requires of us – faith. If we haven't figured it out already, the false truths are in complete opposition with God's word. God is for you, not against you.

"HIS LOVE CANNOT BE BROKEN; HIS GRACE IS UNLIMITED; HIS COVERING CANNOT BE PENETRATED; HIS SHIELD OF PROTECTION IS SUFFICIENT FOR EVERY WEAPON."
[#motivated]

Friends, if the Creator of all life is for you, what (and who) can ever be against you? What opposition can succeed against you if God is for you? Nothing! There's no challenge, no storm, no trouble, no hardship, no persecution, no war, no poverty, no danger, no angel, no demon, no fear, no worry, no sickness, no disease, no powers of darkness, no famine, no pestilence, no plague, no disaster, no creation that can succeed against you. Nothing can succeed against us if God is for us. Good news, He is for you! HE IS FOR YOU! His love cannot be broken; His grace is unlimited; His covering cannot be penetrated [breached, entered]; His shield of protection is sufficient for every weapon; and because of our Savior Jesus Christ (and through Him), we are more than conquerors, which means we are "super-conquerors".

Therefore, it's time for us to make some changes in our lives, beginning with the thoughts that we choose to entertain. Immediately reject and dismiss all false truths. How can we discern a false truth? It always contradicts God's Word and attempts to lead us away from God by shifting the focus on anything other than God, especially ourselves (the "me movement"). We can guarantee that false truths will attempt to enter our lives during challenging times of vulnerability, loss, grief, breakups, loneliness, weakness, emptiness, brokenness, and uncertainty. This is when we must remember that our God is for us and His love for us is more than enough. Remember, He's the Creator, the Way Maker, the Almighty, Omnipotent, Omniscient, Perfect God that leads, guides, and directs our path. So, let's shift the focus away from the challenges in and around our lives, and focus on His love for us. Remember, He is for you!

DEFINE THE PROBLEM | DEVELOP THE SOLUTION

Think about a time that you messed up. I mean really messed up and thought that God would never forgive you. Were you right or wrong? Obviously, you were wrong because you're still reading this message right now, which means God forgave you and spared you from His wrath at that time. Don't allow manipulation and deception to steer you away from God. Always repent for the mistakes and bad choices and allow God's love to unite you with Him. Here's a quick prayer for you, "Father, please help me to not give in to the lies and deceiving voices that attempt to break my relationship with You. Help me to always guard my thoughts and my heart. Help me to stay under Your covering and protection because that's where I belong. In Jesus' Name I pray. Amen."

ENCOURAGEMENT OF THE WEEK [#truth]

Is there a greater source of truth than God? God is the Source for all life, so we must remember to never doubt God, for when we do, we accept false truths as valid information. If we can't trust God, is there anything or anyone we can trust? Absolutely not! Trust God with your everything and know that He is for you.

SPREAD THE MOTIVATION [#motivate]

Encourage someone that's battling condemnation to know that God's love for us extends beyond the mistakes and bad choices. Repentance is the path, Jesus Christ is the bridge, and God is the embracing Father.

Week 38 Motivation

LOOK BACK

∞ ∞ ∞

Exodus 13:3 [NLT]

*So, Moses said to the people, "This is a day to remember forever—the day you left Egypt, the place of your slavery. Today the L*ORD *has brought you out by the power of His mighty hand. (Remember, eat no food containing yeast.)*

Dear Friends,

How many times have you looked back to see where you were going? That question doesn't make much sense, right? How can looking back help us to see what's ahead? As you know, the title of this message is "Look Back", which means we'll probably be able to find out very soon. Most biblical messages that we hear and read will almost certainly involve us looking forward and moving forward, but not looking back. What if I told you that for us to move forward, we must look back? Remember the year 2020? Yes, you remember 2020. It's the year that will be forever etched in the history books, as it was the year that the world was changed because of the pandemic. We all can attest to the fact that 2020 was one-of-a-kind. If someone would've told us in advance what to expect in 2020, I'm not sure any of us would've believed it. It was a very challenging year, a very disturbing year, and a year filled with emotional discomfort. However, it was also a year of grace, favor, and prosperity. Yes, you read that last statement correctly. For us to see what transpired throughout the year, we must look back.

In the featured scripture, Moses told the people to always remember the day that they left Egypt. Egypt represented the place of their slavery, the place of bondage and hardship, and the place of challenges and emotional discomfort. If we take it a step further, Egypt also represented the place where they met God's grace, favor, and prosperity. Hard to fathom, right? Let's connect the dots. In Exodus 2:23-24, we read that the Israelites continued to groan under their burden of slavery, and they cried out for help, and finally their cry rose up to God. In other words, God heard them crying continuously for His help. God remembered His covenant with Abraham, Isaac, and Jacob, and decided that it was time to act. Their hardship met God's grace. If we fast-forward to Exodus 12, we'll learn that Pharaoh had enough and released the Israelites from bondage, but the story didn't stop there. Check out verses 35-36, which says, "And the people of Israel did as Moses had instructed; they asked the Egyptians for clothing and articles of silver and gold.

The LORD caused the Egyptians to look favorably on the Israelites, and they gave the Israelites whatever they asked for. So, they stripped the Egyptians of their wealth!". Do you see the result? Favor and prosperity. Their hardship met God's grace and resulted in favor and prosperity.

> *"IT'S NOT BY CHANCE, NOR LUCK, NOR HAPPENSTANCE, NOR BY THE UNIVERSE'S MYSTICAL POWERS OR "ENERGY" THAT YOU'RE STILL ALIVE TODAY. IT'S BY THE GRACE, FAVOR, AND PROSPERITY OF GOD."*
> *[#motivated]*

Friends, if we can learn anything from this story, it's that God's grace, favor, and prosperity is on the other side of hardship and challenges. Here's something new to note >>> faith requires us to remember (Look Back!). For us to put our faith in God, we must remember who He is and what He has done (Look Back!). Sure, 2020 was filled with hardships, problems, challenges, grief, loss, storms, disappointment, anger, and every other negative emotion that we can think of, but if you are able to read or listen to this message now, that means God's grace met you in a great time of need. That means you were covered and protected from an outcome that could've ended your life on earth. That means God remembered you. Now, it's time for us to remember God. It's time for us to look back! Look back at this year, 2020, and all the years that you were fortunate to live and see what God has done for you, in you, and with you. It's not by chance, nor luck, nor happenstance, nor by the universe's mystical powers or "energy" that you're still alive today. It's by the grace, favor, and prosperity of God. God kept you from destruction. God saved you from the fatal storm. God rescued you from bondage. God delivered us all from the hardships of Egypt (remember what Egypt represented). Sure, we've had trouble, we've had our patience tested and stretched beyond what we could've imagined, we've battled various conflicting emotions all at once, and we've experienced great loss, but you know what else? Through God, we've endured and persevered, which means we've prospered. 2020 and every year that we've made it through was a year of grace, favor, and prosperity.

To truly see the truth, don't limit your focus on the material or tangible things. You've prospered in grace. You've prospered in endurance and perseverance. You've prospered in God's love and the never-ending peace of Christ. FYI, this is a perfect time to praise God for your prosperity [*insert praise here*]. We must continue to prosper in faith, hope, belief, trust, love, peace, and all of the other uplifting Christ-like characteristics. As we prepare for new days ahead, let's not forget to look back and see what God has done in our individual lives. Let's remember who He is and what He has done, and carry that elevating faith into each year and all of the days ahead. Look back!

DEFINE THE PROBLEM | DEVELOP THE SOLUTION

Think about a time that you cried out to God for help and didn't receive an immediate answer. What did you do? No matter what happened it was an opportunity to learn. Now, you can look back and learn from the success and failures of the past. If you didn't receive an immediate answer, it's because God had a plan, and He still has a plan. Trust Him to provide you His sufficient grace. Here's a quick prayer for you, "Father, please help me to remember that your grace is always sufficient for me. I don't know everything, and I'll never know everything, but I can trust You to give me the answers I need in life. Show me the way and guide me along Your paths for the rest of my life. In Jesus' Name I pray. Amen."

ENCOURAGEMENT OF THE WEEK [#prosperity]

When prosperity is mentioned, physical riches and wealth generally come to mind, but there's more to prosperity than that. Peace, joy, salvation, wisdom, love, and favor are some of the many things that can cause a person to be prosperous and successful. Don't limit God's ability to prosper you in every area of your life.

SPREAD THE MOTIVATION [#motivate]

Encourage someone to look back and remember all the things that God did for them and saved them from and let them know that God is still doing what He always does; He's extending His sufficient grace.

Week 39 Motivation

NOT ALONE

∞ ∞ ∞

Ecclesiastes 3:1 [NIV]
There is a time for everything, and a season for every activity under the heavens.

Dear Friends,

What's your favorite season of the year? Depending on where you're currently located (geographically), you may experience various types of seasons. What if I told you that the same concept applies to our lives? It's true! We will experience different types of seasons depending on where we're currently at in life. In other words, the seasons that we experience depends on the level that we're currently on. Think about a challenging video game that has different levels to go through as part of the overall storyline. That's like our lives on Earth. We have levels that we must go through, and each level presents its own difficult challenges. What is a season? A season is a period that usually has a start date and an end date. Seasons produce change and faith-building opportunities. Seasons cause people to enter and exit our lives. Seasons cause responsibilities to increase with time. Seasons produce times of fruitful abundance and times of adversity. If we're not equipped with faith in God, seasons can be deceiving, causing us to accept uncertainty, doubt, and a false belief that that there's no end date for the difficulty that we face. Good news! It doesn't matter what season we're in, we'll never be alone. Why? Because we have a perfect Lord and Savior in Jesus Christ that is with us every step of the way. Yes, we're not alone.

> *"ACCEPT GOD'S SUFFICIENT GRACE FOR EVERY TIME IN YOUR LIFE. THE RIGHT TIME IS GOD'S TIME!"*
> *[#motivated]*

Friends, no matter what season you're currently in, consider it an opportunity to grow even more in your faith, trust, belief, and hope in Jesus Christ. Accept God's sufficient grace for every season and time in your life. The right time is God's time. During trying times, His grace is sufficient. During difficult times, His grace is sufficient. During testing times, His grace is sufficient. During good times, bad times, end times, every time, no matter the time, His grace is sufficient. One of the most popular Bible quotes is found in 2 Corinthians 12:9, which says, "But He said to me, "My grace is sufficient for you, for My power is made perfect in weakness (NIV)." If we start at the beginning of the chapter, we'll read a story about a time that the Apostle Paul was in a season of difficulty. He was being tormented continuously by a messenger of the Adversary (Satan), in what he described as a thorn in his flesh. He pleaded with God on numerous occasions to take it away from him, but God reminded him of His sufficient grace. As we continue to verse 10, we'll discover that Paul has learned a valuable lesson and has realized the positive (+) in the negative (-) from this experience, as he said, "That is why, for Christ's sake, I delight in weaknesses, in insults, in hardships, in persecutions, in difficulties. For when I am weak, then I am strong (NIV)".

Friends, with God, there's always a positive (+) in the negative (-). The season may change, the level of difficulty may change, the things around us may change, but His sufficient grace will always remain the same and it'll always be sufficient for us. Always! Therefore, take heart, be encouraged, and know that you're never alone. Although it may not seem like it, there's a lesson that can be learned in every season. Here are a few lessons for each of us to remember: (1) God's grace will always be sufficient for us, no matter what we're going through; (2) when we are weak, we are strong through Jesus Christ; and (3) we're never alone if we allow Jesus Christ to accompany us for the rest of our lives. Let this season and every season that follows be filled with the unlimited love and irrevocable [permanent, irreversible] peace that only Jesus Christ can give us. Remember, you're not alone.

DEFINE THE PROBLEM | DEVELOP THE SOLUTION

Think about a time when you were in a lengthy season of difficulty. How did things change for you? The answer is God's grace! Even when it doesn't seem as if God is answering our prayers or paying attention to us, be fully assured that He's always with us. The storms and the seasons can't take away His love for us. Remember that as you go through the different seasons in life. Here's a quick prayer for you, "Father, please help me to remember that I'm never alone in life because You are always with me. In the tough times, trying times, and challenging times, You are always with me. Help me to never forget Your love for me. I choose to live for You forever. In Jesus' Name I pray. Amen."

ENCOURAGEMENT OF THE WEEK [#grace]

God's grace is perfect, unlimited, and is always enough. It's enough when the problems are great, when the possibilities are limited, and when the opposition surrounds us. Trust Him to always supply His sufficient grace in every season that you face.

SPREAD THE MOTIVATION [#motivate]

Encourage someone to trust God and not focus on the season. Help them to focus on God's grace. Changes will occur with seasons, but God's grace will endure and withstand everything.

Week 40 Motivation
Patiently Waiting

∞ ∞ ∞

Psalm 27:14 [NLT]
Wait patiently for the Lord. Be brave and courageous. Yes, wait patiently for the Lord.

Dear Friends,

If you were asked to rate your level of patience from a scale of 0-10, what would your level be? It's safe to assume that half of Earth's population would be at 5 or lower. Why? Because most of us have children and/or have had our daily lives impacted by children [*insert laughter here*]. Just joking. Maybe it's because we generally want what we want when we want it, which causes us to not want to wait. If we do wait, we often prefer not to wait too long. Unfortunately for us, those that choose to submit to, surrender to, and obey God must master the art of patience or else continue to experience disappointment and unmet expectations because God doesn't operate according to our timeline. Patience is extremely important and beneficial for each of us, and it's also one of the most difficult things to maintain over time. A few close friends of patience are hope, faith, endurance, perseverance, tolerance, resilience, persistence, and diligence. These are all traits that God's children should have in common.

In the featured scripture, we're able to receive guidance from an individual that had first-hand experience of the need for patience. This individual is David. If you're not familiar with the life story of David, read the books of Samuel (1 Samuel & 2 Samuel). In fact, if we read the life story of David, we'll notice that he was anointed to be king of Israel in 1 Samuel 16, but he didn't become king over all Israel until 2 Samuel 5 (several years had passed). While waiting for the appointed kingship, David endured a lot of difficult times, including having to flee from the jealous king that he served because the king wanted to kill him. This jealous king was also the father of David's wife (Michal) and the father of his best friend (Jonathan), whom he considered a brother. We can get a glimpse of David's heart from reading the different Psalms that he wrote. So, when we read "Wait patiently for the Lord. Be brave and courageous. Yes, wait patiently for the Lord", we can arrive at the conclusion that waiting patiently on God requires a level of bravery and courage because of the different events that could occur while waiting.

> *"OUR LOVE FOR GOD IS A SELFLESS LOVE COMPRISED OF FAITH, TRUST, OBEDIENCE, SUBMISSION, SURRENDERING, AND WAITING."*
> *[#motivated]*

Friends, patience is not easy, and waiting on the LORD is probably even more difficult than simply having patience. God's timing is not always clear to us, and sometimes it may seem as if we're stuck in a period of uncertainty and waiting confusingly for some kind of clue or direction. Sometimes, God's direction is the promise that He provided us long ago. Choosing to live for God requires the type of faith that says, "I may not be aware of the complete directions, but I know that God will never steer me in the wrong direction". When we choose to patiently wait on God, we choose to deny ourselves, including our wants and desires. We choose to surrender to God's plan and will for us. There may be a lot of times when we do not want to do what God wants us to do, especially wait for an extended period, but it's important to remember that He has all of the answers. He knows why, when, and how (and who, what, where as well). Keep in mind, there may be more times that you don't want to wait on God compared to the times that you do want to wait on Him, but the key word to focus on is "want". Submitting to, surrendering to, and obeying God overrides the "want" factor. We may want to do something, but if it's not what God instructs us to do, then it doesn't matter what we want. That's what love does. It makes sacrifices.

Have you ever allowed your love for someone to cause you to do things that you didn't want to do, but you did, and it brought joy to the other person? Before you answer that one, no, I'm not talking about anything illegal or sinful. I'm talking about something like giving a foot massage to a spouse after a long day, or pausing the sports game or talk show to hear about your children's day at school, or buying a small gift just because you knew it would bless a loved one. Those simple acts of love represent sacrifice. Sacrifice requires selflessness to be at the forefront of our decisions and at the center of our heart. That's what our relationship with God should look like. Our relationship with God must be filled with selfless love that's comprised of faith, trust, obedience, submission, surrendering, and waiting. Waiting patiently on Him is the key. We must learn to trust God's timing, even when we don't understand why. As is the case with any relationship, trust is the baseline for our relationship with God and our Lord and Savior Jesus Christ. Therefore, let's choose to live selfless lives filled with complete trust in God. Be brave and courageous as you patiently wait on God.

DEFINE THE PROBLEM | DEVELOP THE SOLUTION

Think about the things that God is telling you to patiently wait on Him for and choose to maintain self-control, which will help you avoid impulsive decisions. Even though it may be difficult to do, trust that God has a perfect plan for you. Here's a quick prayer for you, "Father, please help me to humbly submit and surrender my complete life to You. Fill me with the level of self-control that I need to live a life that reflects my Lord and Savior Jesus Christ. I commit to changing my thoughts, my actions, and my words. Help me to trust Your timing, Your plan, and Your will, and help me to remember that You're always in full control. In Jesus' Name I pray. Amen."

ENCOURAGEMENT OF THE WEEK [#patience]

Patience can be one of the most peaceful things in life. It can give us a level of calmness that will steer us along the green pastures of peace. It's a gift of strength that God has purposely designed for us to have, so let's get it and keep it.

SPREAD THE MOTIVATION [#motivate]

Encourage someone to trust in the LORD even though their current circumstances may not be the best. He has us covered, always!

Week 41 Motivation
TRUST AND BELIEVE

∞ ∞ ∞

John 14:1 [NLT]
"Don't let your hearts be troubled. Trust in God, and trust also in Me."

Dear Friends,

How much do you trust and believe in God? I know it's an unexpected question, but it's a question that may cause us to evaluate ourselves a bit more clearly and accurately. We may say that we trust and believe in God, but different situations often introduce caveats [stipulations, conditions]. For instance, we can say that we trust God completely, but then an unexpected event occurs that seems too impossible to not happen the way it usually would, and we believe that the result will be the same. Is that complete trust? No, it's called trusting with caveats. What if your relationship with your spouse had certain caveats, like "I'll trust you as long as you cook for me" or "I'll trust you as long as you pay my bills" or "I'll trust you as long as you keep your job"? Doesn't sound like real trust, does it? Well, when we choose to place stipulations and conditions on God, we're essentially doing the same thing. If you're wondering, any relationship that's built on conditional trust is not sustainable [it won't last]. Our relationship with God is no different, and that's where the featured scripture comes into practice. Jesus recognized that the disciples had different emotions, some more troubling than others. Why? If we go back to John 13, we'll see the reason. In chapter 13, Jesus predicted His betrayal, and notified the disciples that He would be going away, and they wouldn't be able to follow Him at that time. Of course, this troubled the disciples, which is why He said the comforting words that we read in John 14. Although those words were spoken to a certain group of individuals at the time, those words are very appropriate for us today.

"WE MAY NOT BE ABLE TO ESCAPE OR CONTROL LIFE'S CHALLENGES, BUT WE CAN BE FULLY PREPARED TO RESPOND TO THEM."
[#motivated]

Friends, throughout the course of life each of us will experience different emotions, including emotions that trouble our heart. It's in those times that we must remember to trust and believe in God and in our Lord and Savior Jesus Christ. We may not be able to escape or control life's challenges, but we can be fully prepared to respond to them. We can be fully equipped to endure and persevere. We can be fully able to overcome all things that we encounter. How? Through our unconditional trust and belief in God. This means trusting God no matter what happens in life. This means trusting God when we're experiencing days of sunshine and days of rain. This means not allowing our problems to dictate our faith. This means remembering that God is in full control and being fully assured that He'll always be in full control

So, don't attempt to take matters into your own hands; place everything in His hands. Everything! Including the things we often try to hold on to as a means of protection. Most of the time, we're unaware that the protection that we thought we had is partially the reason for the troubling thoughts, the overwhelming feelings of anxiety, the peace-stealing fear, and every other concern that plays a factor in us placing conditions and stipulations on our trust and belief in God. If your level of trust in God is based on how well life is going for you, that's a clear indication that you're a major storm away from no longer trusting God. If we continue to read John 14, we'll see that Jesus said, "Peace I leave with you; My [perfect] peace I give to you; not as the world gives do I give to you. Do not let your heart be troubled, nor let it be afraid. [Let My perfect peace calm you in every circumstance and give you courage and strength for every challenge.]" (John 14:28, AMP). Let's choose to trust and believe in Jesus and know that we're covered by God and are filled with the perfect peace of our Savior Jesus Christ.

DEFINE THE PROBLEM | DEVELOP THE SOLUTION

Think about a time that you had no choice but to trust God and believe that He would do the thing that you needed to be done. You reached a point of desperation, and it was that desperation that required a deeper level of faith. Remember that and don't forget it. Don't forget that desperate faith, hope, belief, and trust in God will lead to God moving on your behalf to do what needs to be done. Keep trusting! Here's a quick prayer for you, "Father, please help me to always trust in You. Let my trust not be conditional or filled with limitations. Let my trust in You be unshakeable, unconditional, and unending. Help me to be Yours forever. In Jesus' Name I pray. Amen."

ENCOURAGEMENT OF THE WEEK [#obedience]

All relationships require trust. This trust must be durable and persistent, and it must remain throughout challenges and difficulties. It's no difference with our relationship with God. If we desire to have a sustainable relationship with God, we must trust Him unconditionally and without limitation. Trusting God is equivalent to declaring your selfless devotion to Him, so let Him know that you're devoted to Him.

SPREAD THE MOTIVATION [#motivate]

Encourage someone to trust God no matter what occurs in life. Let them know that it's through trusting in God that we're able to be recipients of His covering, protection, and blessings.

Week 42 Motivation

VICTORY

∞ ∞ ∞

1 Corinthians 5:4-5 [NLT]
For every child of God defeats this evil world, and we achieve this victory through our faith. And who can win this battle against the world? Only those who believe that Jesus is the Son of God.

Dear Friends,

Are you aware of the fact that battles are a constant part of life? Sure, we have the competitive battles in sports and in different contests, and I can't forget to mention the toughest of all, which is family game night. FYI, if you don't currently do family game night, perhaps it's for the better because they almost always end in someone saying, "you're cooking your own dinner" when the loser is the preparer of dinner [*insert laughter here*]. Even though those battles are tough, there are much greater battles in life. Many individuals have distinct battles with health, addiction, behavior, and sin. These battles, especially the battle with sin, can be very difficult for individuals to overcome on their own. If I'm being completely honest with you, it's impossible for us to overcome anything on our own. We will always require God's intervention [involvement, interference], even when we don't realize it. God created us to have full reliance and dependence on Him. He's omniscient [knows everything], omnipresent [always present], and is in full control of everything.

To paint a simple picture for you, let's imagine this scenario >>> you decide to purchase a lot of action figures that you'll use to build your small fictional [imaginary, not unreal] village. As the creator of this village, you're in control of everything that happens in the village and in the lives of each action figure. Nothing can be said or done without you knowing. And nothing can happen without your final consent [approval, permission], not even weather changes, why? Because you're in full control. Do you see the big picture? The creator of the creation always knows everything about everything. If you haven't made the connection yet, this is how it is with God. The key difference is, His creation extends beyond a small village and covers an entire world, universe, galaxy, and everything else that exists. He's in full control of it all. All, meaning everything, everyone, and every matter. This includes the individual battles that each of us experience in life.

"VICTORY BELONGS TO JESUS AND EVERYONE THAT CHOOSE TO TRUST AND BELIEVE IN HIM."
[#motivated]

Friends, until the world as we know it ceases to exist, there will always be a battle between right and wrong, good and bad, righteousness and sin. Everything that is good comes from God and is a symbol of His love. Everything that is bad does not come from God, but is derived from Satan (aka the devil). Since the fall of Adam and Eve, evil has infiltrated [intruded, gained entry] and influenced the world. In fact, when we hear or read about biblical references to the "world", it's referencing sin, evil, and everything that's considered bad; all of which oppose God. There's a reason why Jesus said, "Wide is the gate and broad is the road that leads to destruction, and many enter through it" (Matthew 7:13, NIV). The world and all that it represents is the popular default choice. Why? We cannot win the battle against the world without God, thus many people who choose to live apart from God is overcome by the world. The featured scripture says, every child of God defeats this evil world and achieves victory through faith in Jesus Christ, the Son of God.

If you're in the battle against the world without faith in Jesus Christ, you're fighting a battle that you can't win. You can choose to be relentless in your pursuit of victory, but without Jesus, defeat is inevitable [it will happen]. However, through faith in Jesus, victory is yours. This means that everything that the world has in its arsenal [collection of weapons] to throw at you will be defeated. Every child of God defeats the world. If Jesus Christ is an active presence in your life, you are a child of God with guaranteed victory. Victory belongs to Jesus and everyone that choose to trust and believe in Him. Let's walk in victory in every facet [aspect] of life, including health, finances, relationships, conduct, and most importantly our everyday life with Jesus.

DEFINE THE PROBLEM | DEVELOP THE SOLUTION

Think about a time when you were in a very difficult battle, and a loss appeared inevitable, but somehow, you overcame the difficulty and won the battle. Think about the strength and the relief that you felt afterwards. It wasn't a coincidence, it was God. God gives His children victory through Jesus Christ. Remember that if/when you experience adversity and difficult challenges. Here's a quick prayer for you, "Father, please help me to always remember that You are in full control of everything that happens in my life. There's no challenge too great for You, so please help me to never limit Your ability. Help me to persevere through all obstacles, roadblocks, and challenges with the help and guidance of my Lord and Savior Jesus Christ. And may my heart and actions always bring You glory. In Jesus' Name I pray. Amen."

ENCOURAGEMENT OF THE WEEK [#perseverance]

Not giving up when things get tough is one of the most rewarding choices possible. In fact, perseverance is more than a choice, it's a characteristic trait. Let perseverance be one of the defining characteristic traits that define you. FYI, it's also a gift of strength from God.

SPREAD THE MOTIVATION [#motivate]

Encourage someone to not give up or give in when difficulty arises. Help them to remember that the gift of perseverance can help them overcome anything in life.

Week 43 Motivation
But God!

∞ ∞ ∞

Genesis 50:20 [GNT]
You plotted evil against me, but God turned it into good, in order to preserve the lives of many people who are alive today because of what happened.

Dear Friends,

Have you ever experienced a "But God!" moment? A good question to ask at this time is, what exactly is a "But God!" moment? It's one of those moments when it seems as if everything is going wrong, in which there are challenges upon challenges upon challenges, and hardship upon hardship, but God intervenes [interfere, intercede] and provides much needed rescue. The Bible is filled with several "But God!" moments. Let's focus on one of the important "But God!" moments that's featured in the story of Joseph, which is found in the book of Genesis. Jealousy and anger led to Joseph being sold into slavery by his brothers for twenty shekels of silver (approximately eight ounces), which also included years of imprisonment. Yes, you heard that correctly, his brothers sold him into slavery to some Ishmaelite/Midianite traders for what would've been a couple months' worth of wages because of jealousy and anger. Joseph's father loved him more than the rest of the brothers and they hated him because of it. Joseph went from freedom in his father's household to being confined in an Egyptian prison where the king's prisoners were confined, all while being innocent. This could have been the end of Joseph, But God!

God intervened, and at the age of thirty, this is what happened to Joseph, "'You shall be in charge of my palace, and all my people are to submit to your orders. Only with respect to the throne will I be greater than you.' So, Pharaoh said to Joseph, 'I hereby put you in charge of the whole land of Egypt.' Then Pharaoh took his signet ring from his finger and put it on Joseph's finger. He dressed him in robes of fine linen and put a gold chain around his neck. He had him ride in a chariot as his second-in-command, and people shouted before him, 'Make way!' Thus, he put him in charge of the whole land of Egypt" (Genesis 41:40-43, NIV).

*"**GOD IS GREATER THAN ANY AND EVERY CHALLENGE THAT CONFRONTS YOU. HE CAN TURN THE NEGATIVE INTO A POSITIVE.**"*
[#motivated]

Friends, do you understand the significance of the events that took place? Joseph spent an extended period in slavery and years in prison after being accused of something that he did not do, but God intervened at the appropriate time, and Joseph went from being a prisoner in the Egyptian king's prison to overseeing the whole land of Egypt. An important part of the Joseph story is the fact that the LORD was with him every step of the way. There were several "But God!" moments throughout his life. When he was a slave in Potiphar's house, who was one of Pharaoh's officials, he prospered and became in charge of Potiphar's household until being wrongly accused and thrown in prison. When he was in prison, the LORD was with him and the warden put him in charge of all the people that were held in the prison; he was made responsible for everything that was done there and had success in all that he did. Joseph's life trials can be summed up by the featured scripture, "You plotted evil against me, but God turned it into good, in order to preserve the lives of many people who are alive today because of what happened."

There may be some things in your life that were designed to harm you, But God! God is greater than any and every challenge that confronts you. He can turn the negative (-) into a positive (+). What was meant to harm you will be turned into a steppingstone for your path of elevation and success. Don't give up! Don't stop being faithful to God! Keep running the race and keep trusting Him to be exactly who and what He is – your everything! God used Joseph's life occurrences to save many lives, now trust Him to do powerful things with yours as well. The problems, challenges, hardships, and trials may surround you, But God!

DEFINE THE PROBLEM | DEVELOP THE SOLUTION
Think about a particular "But God!" moment that happened in your life. Think about the problem and how it seemed impossible to overcome, but God stepped in and changed everything and made it work in your favor. Think about how that made you feel and the faith and gratitude that you had. Don't forget those times, as you encounter different obstacles in life. Here's a quick prayer for you, "Father, please help me to trust in You, no matter how great the problems are in my life. Help me to remember the many times that You stepped in and saved me and let me trust in Your ability to do it again. I give You my all. In Jesus' Name I pray. Amen."

ENCOURAGEMENT OF THE WEEK [#however]
When we see "however" in a story, we know that things are about to change. If things were going bad, a "however" is an indicator that things changed for the better. That's exactly what happens in our lives. Things may have been difficult or challenging, however, God is who He is, and He will do what He does, and that's turn it all around because of His great love for us.

SPREAD THE MOTIVATION [#motivate]
Encourage someone to not give up on God because of difficulty. Help them to remember that God has perfect timing and a perfect plan that requires us to keep trusting in Him.

Week 44 Motivation

BUT GOD! (PART II)

∞ ∞ ∞

1 Samuel 23:14 [NLT]
David now stayed in the strongholds of the wilderness and in the hill country of Ziph. Saul hunted him day after day, but God didn't let Saul find him.

Dear Friends,

To test your recollection of the previous message, how would you describe a "But God!" moment? It's okay if you forgot the words to properly describe it, I know you were giving your undivided attention while reading the message, so I'll help you out. As we learned from the previous message titled, "But God!", a "But God!" moment is one of those moments when it seems as if everything is going wrong, in which there are challenges upon challenges upon challenges, and hardship upon hardship, but God intervenes [interfere, intercede] and provides much needed rescue. In this message, we'll focus on the life of David and one of the most encouraging "But God!" moments in the Bible. Much like Joseph, the story of David is highlighted by jealousy and anger, but instead of family members being jealous and angry at David, it's his king. What do you do when your king, your appointed leader is jealous of you?

Before we analyze David's response, it's important to recap the events leading up to it. In the early days of the Bible, it was noted that the nation of Israel was one of the very few nations that didn't have an actual king to physically govern the nation. The primary reason for this was because God was their leader, which made a king unnecessary. The people of Israel insisted, so the LORD gave them a king named Saul. While he was king, Saul disobeyed God's direct instructions, which led to God rejecting Saul as king of Israel. God chose David, while he was still in his youth, to be the successor to Saul as king of Israel, primarily because David had a heart of love for God. Several events transpired after David was chosen by God. The most popular event being the big showdown between David and Goliath. David was successful in all that he did because He had the favor of God. This led to an increased amount of fear, jealousy, and anger from Saul towards David, as Saul allowed the negative emotions to consume him. Saul's jealousy of David became so great that Saul treated David as his enemy for the rest of his life and he tried to kill David on multiple occasions. I forgot to mention that David was Saul's son-in-law and best friend of Saul's son Jonathan. Can you say, dilemma?!

David fled Saul and battled loneliness, depression, and distress for an extended period, as Saul continued to pursue him to kill him. Yes, it's fair to state that Saul was very obsessed with David. This could have been the end of David, But God!

"I WON'T STOP BELIEVING, I WON'T STOP HOPING, I WON'T STOP TRUSTING BECAUSE MY GOD IS GREATER, BIGGER, STRONGER, WISER, AND IS THE KING OF KINGS, LORD OF LORDS, AND THE CREATOR OF LIFE".
[#motivated]

Friends, it's not over until God says it's over! God will always have the final say in the matter. David's life seemed to be over, even before he was able to rule as king of Israel. It appeared that he would spend the rest of his life running, fleeing, and hiding from the pursuit of a king and his mighty army. However, he was living in a "But God!" moment. God anointed David to be Saul's successor, which means God placed a specific calling and purpose on David's life. Although David had to go through challenge upon challenge, and hardship upon hardship, God's plan for David superseded [succeeded, overtook] the storms that he experienced. This is encouragement for each of us. When there's a specific calling and purpose for our lives, the storms, challenges, hardship, and difficulty that attempt to come against us, break us, knock us down, or discourage us won't matter. God will intervene and remind us that He's in full control. Sure, we have an enemy in the devil and his demonic army that seek to harm us, distract us, and lead us to destruction, but God! God is greater than any opposition that we face. David went from fleeing and hiding from Saul to becoming king of all Israel. What should have broken David was used to build him up. What should have destroyed David was used to teach him how to have faith and trust in God, no matter the circumstance.

God is calling each of us to have faith and trust in Him. To have the type of faith that helps us stand strong, even when we're surrounded by trouble. The type of faith that refuses to throw in the towel when the hardships of life knock us down. The type of faith that says, "I won't stop believing, I won't stop hoping, I won't stop trusting because my God is greater, bigger, stronger, wiser, and is the King of kings, Lord of lords, and the Creator of life". It doesn't matter what tactic the devil and his army attempt to use against us! If God is for us, there is nothing that can successfully come against us. Not death, not sickness, not famine, not opposition >>>nothing! Therefore, let's be encouraged by the life of David and remember that God is always in control and will always intervene at the right time.

DEFINE THE PROBLEM | DEVELOP THE SOLUTION

Think about a time that you were confused about your path in life? You may not have had an idea of what steps to take or how to begin, but God helped you to see your purpose. Think about how that made you feel and the motivation that you received. The next time that you're tempted to accept discouragement, remember the purpose that God placed on your life and keep pushing. Here's a quick prayer for you, "Father, please help me to remember that I have been called according to Your purpose. Help me to remember that You've already determined my purpose for glorifying You. Even when it seems as if I'm lost or headed in the wrong direction, please help me to remember that You have the final say, always. In Jesus' Name I pray. Amen."

ENCOURAGEMENT OF THE WEEK [#purpose]

Purpose is pre-determined and defined by God. God calls us according to His purpose, according to the purpose He placed on us and in us. When there is purpose for our lives, nothing along the journey will be able to prevent us from achieving it. It doesn't matter how things may seem; God's purpose will always prevail.

SPREAD THE MOTIVATION [#motivate]

Encourage someone to look past the negatives that are seen and focus on the positive assurance of God's purpose for those that love Him unconditionally through the Savior Jesus Christ.

Week 45 Motivation

BUT GOD! (PART III)

∞ ∞ ∞

Acts 3:15 [NLT]
You killed the Author of life, but God raised Him from the dead. And we are witnesses of this fact!

Dear Friends,

What's your favorite personal "But God!" moment? Remember, a "But God!" moment is one of those moments when it seems as if everything is going wrong, in which there are challenges upon challenges upon challenges, and hardship upon hardship, but God intervenes [interfere, intercede] and provide much needed rescue. The most important "But God!" moment is found in the life of Jesus Christ. If you were wondering, the life of Jesus Christ (birth, ministry, death, and resurrection) is the most significant in history. Yes, you read that correctly; it's the most significant in history. The birth of Jesus led to King Herod giving orders to kill all the boys in Bethlehem and in its vicinity [area, region] who were two years old and under, out of fear that Jesus was the Messiah spoken about in history. The ministry of Jesus began with Him being tested in the wilderness by the devil, and continued until His death, which was motivated by the chief priests and elders of the Israelites, out of fear that Jesus was indeed the Son of God and King of the Jews.

Persecution, hatred, fear, jealousy, and intense anger surrounded Jesus throughout His life on earth and those that chose to follow Him. It's no coincidence that this trend has continued thousands of years later. Followers of Jesus are still hated, mocked, and crucified all throughout the world. Jesus knew that this would occur and said the following, "If the world hates you, keep in mind that it hated Me first. If you belonged to the world, it would love you as its own. As it is, you do not belong to the world, but I have chosen you out of the world. That is why the world hates you. Remember what I told you: 'A servant is not greater than his master.' If they persecuted Me, they will persecute you also. If they obeyed My teaching, they will obey yours also" (John 15:18-20, NIV). Following Jesus is not an easy task, But God!

> *"When the storm thinks it has you pinned down for the count, or when the challenges think that you're outnumbered, or when the adversity thinks it has you trapped, the Holy Spirit reminds you that you're not alone."*
>
> *[#motivated]*

Friends, God said it's not over until He says it's over (not literally, but through action). The victory that the enemy thought he had was interrupted by the Resurrected King and Savior Jesus Christ. The enemy celebrated for two days and recognized his doomed fate on the third day when the Messiah, the Son of God, King of the Jews, and now Resurrected Savior "has risen". This is and will always be the biggest "But God!" moment (and "Mic Drop!" moment) in the history of the world. Jesus not only defeated the enemy, but He also defeated sin and death. Noticed what He said in John 16:33, which occurred before the cross, "In this world you will have trouble. But take heart! I have overcome the world" (NIV). He knew well in advance that the "But God!" moment was going to occur, and He prepared everyone for this history-shattering event. What if we possessed that same level of insight? What if we knew we had the promised victory from God and believed it and lived it? Our lives wouldn't be filled with lukewarm faith or part-time love for Jesus, it would be filled with the completeness of Jesus Christ. It would reflect Jesus, and it would be surrendered to Jesus.

Do you understand the point of these 'But God!' messages? It's not about the storms or the challenges that we experience. There will always be some form of adversity for the followers of Jesus, but there will also be a "But God!" moment for each of those experiences. Don't believe me? Have you ever heard about the Holy Spirit? If not, read John 14:15-18, which says, "If you love Me, keep My commands. And I will ask the Father, and He will give you another Advocate to help you and be with you forever—the Spirit of truth. The world cannot accept Him, because it neither sees Him nor knows Him. But you know Him, for He lives with you and will be in you. I will not leave you as orphans; I will come to you" (NIV). That qualifies for a "But God!" moment. When the storm thinks it has you pinned down for the count, or when the challenges think that you're outnumbered, or when the adversity thinks it has you trapped, the Holy Spirit reminds you that you're not alone. Not alone! We are not alone! Jesus Christ is with us and His Spirit lives in us. Now, it's time for us to trust Him, submit to Him, and live for Him. Trouble may occur, But God!

DEFINE THE PROBLEM | DEVELOP THE SOLUTION

Think about your current relationship with the Holy Spirit and how it feels to know that Jesus Christ is always with you. The feeling is like having a very popular well-respected big brother. Live each day knowing that the Savior has given you His Spirit to always be with you and in you. Here's a quick prayer for you, "Father, please help me to remember that I'm not alone in life. No matter how alone I may feel, help me to remember that the Holy Spirit dwells in me because of my relationship with Jesus Christ. Help me to continue to yield to the guidance and influence of the Holy Spirit and help me to be even closer with You. In Jesus' Name I pray. Amen."

ENCOURAGEMENT OF THE WEEK [#follower]

Many people aspire to be leaders, which is a good thing, but the best leader is the follower of Jesus Christ. Jesus is the blueprint for everything in life. There's nothing that He didn't know or couldn't do. If we want to lead, we must first follow Jesus Christ.

SPREAD THE MOTIVATION [#motivate]

Encourage someone to follow Jesus Christ, not temporarily, but for the rest of their lives. Let them know that Jesus Christ is the Way, the Truth, and the Life.

Week 46 Motivation
PUSH

∞ ∞ ∞

Mark 3:10 [NLT]
He had healed many people that day, so all the sick people eagerly pushed forward to touch Him.

Dear Friends,

If I told you that we can learn a lot from the people who were said to be "sick" in the days of Jesus, what would you say? Before you answer, it's important to know that the people who were classified as "sick" had severe skin conditions, severe birth defects, body parts that didn't work, dysfunctional organs and systems, and although not applicable for this message, some even had evil spirits that possessed them. Now that you're fully aware of the conditions that the "sick" people had, what would you say? If I'm being completely honest with you, it's difficult to think that we can learn anything from someone classified as "sick" in those days, but God! God uses the world around us to teach us and help us grow. Think about it. How many times have you learned from something bad? Most of the time, we look at the bad and learn what not to do, but not in this case. It's the opposite. We can look at the bad and learn what to do. After that last sentence, you may be tempted to skip this message and tune it out of your short-term memory, but there's a valuable lesson to learn that we're about to get to. Look at what the "sick" people did in the featured scripture. They pushed forward to touch Jesus. They refused to give up. They refused to allow the hardship of life to prevent and restrict them from getting to Jesus. They pushed forward. So, what can we learn and what should we do? If the "sick" people pushed forward, limitations and all, what should the healthy and well do?

"LET NOTHING PREVENT YOU FROM TOUCHING JESUS. JESUS IS BEFORE YOU LEADING THE PATH AND ESTABLISHING THE FOOTSTEPS FOR YOU TO FOLLOW IN."
[#motivated]

Friends, we must push! Push forward and don't stop! Life can be difficult, very difficult at times. This is true for those that don't have a relationship with Jesus Christ, and true for those of us that do have a relationship with Jesus Christ. The point is that challenges are an essential part of life. Some of the most valuable lessons occur during these challenges. If the "sick" people during the days of Jesus had not experienced those difficulties, would they have known how to push past the obstacles and push forward to get to Jesus? If you had been granted everything that you wanted when you wanted it, would you have known how to be relentless in prayer or how to pray until something happens? (Just in case you missed what just happened with that last sentence, "P.U.S.H." is the universally accepted acronym for "pray until something happens").

Whatever you're going through now, don't let it stop you. Your unlimited strength is found in the Savior Jesus Christ, and He will propel you forward. Consider Isaiah 43:1-2 in which God's message was delivered to His people in Israel, as it says, "Do not be afraid, for I have ransomed you. I have called you by name; you are Mine. When you go through deep waters, I will be with you. When you go through rivers of difficulty, you will not drown. When you walk through the fire of oppression, you will not be burned up; the flames will not consume you" (NLT). These words were applicable to His children in the days of old, and they're applicable to His children today. God will not abandon you. He is with you! You have been called by name, and you are His. He'll be with you in the deep waters, which includes those hectic times of uncertainty that seek to strip you of your peace, but can't. He'll be with you through the rivers of difficulty, which includes the ruthless storms that are designed to destroy you, but can't. He'll be with you through the fire of oppression, which includes the various tactics of persecution that are designed to break you, but can't. God will be with you through it all. Therefore, you must push! Push forward and keep on moving. Let nothing prevent you from touching Jesus. Jesus is before you leading the path and establishing the footsteps for you to follow in. All you have to do is push, so let's keep pushing.

DEFINE THE PROBLEM | DEVELOP THE SOLUTION

Think about a time that you were defeated, broken (emotionally, mentally, or even physically), or suffered hardship. You're still here today, so how did you do it? Did you trust God to get you through it or did you do everything on your own? Even when we think we're doing everything on our own, it's God's grace granting us permission to do it. So, the point is, trust God to get you through everything that you face, no matter the level of difficulty. Here's a quick prayer for you, "Father, please help me to not give up when the difficulties of life confront me. Help me to remember that You have given me endurance to withstand, and perseverance to overcome the challenges. I trust in You and in Your ability to help me in every step I take. Thank You for being My Father and for allowing me to have Jesus Christ as my only Lord and Savior. In Jesus' Name I pray. Amen."

ENCOURAGEMENT OF THE WEEK [#push]

To push means to keep going. To keep moving forward, even when obstacles and challenges are sent your way to stop you or block you from reaching the next level. God gives each of the ability and endurance to keep moving forward through Him.

SPREAD THE MOTIVATION [#motivate]

Encourage someone to avoid giving up and throwing in the towel. The difficulties of life produce the greatest resiliency at times, when God is in the picture.

Week 47 Motivation

BREAK DOWN THE WALLS

∞ ∞ ∞

John 4
(Jesus Talks with a Samaritan Woman)

Dear Friends,

Can you think of two groups that absolutely hate or despise each other? Perhaps, you immediately thought about U.S. politics where there are the democrats and republicans. The disdain for one another appears to be serious and sad. How sad? Matthew 12:25 sad (every house divided against itself will not stand). Many of us have heard the popular Bible story about Jesus talking with the Samaritan woman at the well. What may not have been made clear is the level of disdain and hatred that the Jews and the Samaritans had towards each other. This dislike for each other originated in the early B.C. days. One of the primary causes of the tension stemmed from the specific location of worship, meaning the place where the temple of God was located. The hatred between the two groups increased even more because the Jews believed the dedicated place to worship was Jerusalem, but the Samaritans believed that Mount Gerizim was the dedicated place, which was outlined in their version of the Torah, known as the Samaritan Pentateuch. Thus, both groups considered the other group's worship illegitimate, mostly because of location. In addition to location, it's rumored that the Jews also questioned the ethnic origin of the Samaritans due to instances of intermingling [mixture, combining] that took place with the Samaritans and Assyrians, and this ultimately caused the Jews to reject the Samaritans as true descendants of Israel.

So, for many years, hatred for a particular ethnic group was passed down from generation to generation (sounds familiar, right?). It was taught in households, it was learned in communities, and it was clearly understood, "have nothing to do with those people!". The "why" wasn't as important as the "must". Fast-forward to today, hatred and disdain for people that are different than us is very much present in the world. There's hatred because of skin color, physical appearance, ethnicity and origin, primary language, religious affiliation, wealth status, and the list goes on and on. We, as human beings, are extremely creative and have developed various reasons to dislike other groups of people that are different than us and we often develop justification for why our feelings are appropriate, but what would Jesus do?

"One encounter with Jesus Christ can break down the walls, break every chain, and restore love across the land".
[#motivated]

Friends, what would Jesus do? We have our answer in the scenario of Jesus conversing with the woman at the well. If we read the entire story, we'll notice that Jesus initiated the conversation by asking the woman for a drink of water. If we pay even more attention to the story, we'll notice that Jesus never received an actual drink of water, which highlights that water wasn't His true reason for being at the well at that point. (Fun Fact: The Samaritan woman dropped her water jar and ran to the village to tell everyone about Jesus, which means neither Jesus nor the woman received water from the well, but the well was the place of their encounter.). Jesus wasn't there to get water; He was there to break down the wall of hatred, disdain, racism, and prejudice that existed between two groups of people that desired to serve God. If we fast-forward to verses 39-42, we'll notice that many Samaritans believed and confessed that He was indeed the Savior of the world. A conversation with one woman led to the removal of a barrier that existed for generations and led to the salvation of many. What happened because of this occurrence? Check out Acts 8:25, which says, "After testifying and preaching the Word of the Lord in Samaria, Peter and John returned to Jerusalem. And they stopped in many Samaritan villages along the way to preach the Good News" (NLT). The Good News was preached to the Samaritans, the former enemies of the Jews.

One encounter with Jesus Christ can break down the walls, break every chain, and restore love across the land. Jesus is the Answer, the Solution, and the Blueprint. If we want to truly solve the pandemic of hatred, disdain, racism, and prejudice because of differences, let's invite Jesus Christ into our hearts and allow Him to remain in our lives for the rest of our lives. Jesus can break the generational cycle. Jesus can bridge the gap. Jesus can establish and sustain the relationship. Jesus is willing and able, and we must let go and let Him in. Say that a few times out loud, "we must let go and let Him in". Sure, the wrongs that have occurred in the past will be forever etched [engraved, carved] in history, but new history can be made as well. The Jews and Samaritans went from enemies who reportedly persecuted each other at times (maybe a lot), to becoming true neighbors and brothers/sisters in Christ. We can't reverse the horrors of slavery, or the countless scenarios of injustice, or the senseless killings of our brothers/sisters, but we can choose to respond with love and allow Jesus to break down the walls. Let's break down the walls through our Lord and Savior Jesus Christ.

DEFINE THE PROBLEM | DEVELOP THE SOLUTION

Think about a time that you possessed a negative bias, hatred, or prejudice towards another person or group of people. Think about why you felt that way and if that benefitted you in any way? Holding onto anger and hatred takes away life, while love promotes life. To truly move past all negative outlooks, love must be at the forefront, leading the way. So, let love be the driving force in your life, each day. Here's a quick prayer for you, "Father, please help me to let go of all my negative views of people that are different than me. Help me to love others despite our differences. Help me to truly represent my Lord and Savior Jesus Christ and lead with love. Let love continue to be my motive. In Jesus' Name I pray. Amen."

ENCOURAGEMENT OF THE WEEK [#love]

Love is the cure for generational hatred. Love sees past differences, previous history, and recent hurt. It doesn't stop because of offenses; it extends beyond borders. Love is what we're called to have and called to do. Let love lead the way.

SPREAD THE MOTIVATION [#motivate]

Encourage someone to break down the barriers of hatred stored in their heart and mind, as they choose to allow love to lead the way each day.

Week 48 Motivation

WHAT DO I DO WHEN MY BACK IS AGAINST THE WALL?

∞ ∞ ∞

Psalm 31:3 [NLT]
You are my Rock and my Fortress. For the honor of Your Name, lead me out of this danger.

Dear Friends,

Have you ever been faced with a dilemma that made you question your next move? Sometimes we're placed in situations where our backs are against the wall (figuratively, not literally). The situations in which our resources won't cover the costs, our supply isn't sufficient, our possibilities are minimal, and the probabilities are unlikely, so what else can we do? We do what we're called to do; we rely and depend on God. We turn to Him and ask for help. He's our Rock and Fortress that will provide us guidance and lead us out of trouble. If we put our complete trust in Him, we'll never be put to shame. For the sake of His Name, He'll lead and guide us out of the dilemma that confronts us. He's the faithful Father that will care for His children, His sons and daughters, when we call on Him in times of trouble, famine, hardship, and/or uncertainty. He's the Provider and Deliverer that will pull our backs off the wall. We can't completely trust in our resources, but we can always trust in our Source for life and our Savior Jesus Christ.

> *"EVERY PROBLEM HAS A SOLUTION, BUT SOME SOLUTIONS CAUSE MORE PROBLEMS. THE BEST SOLUTION FOR US IS GOD'S SOLUTION."*
> *[#motivated]*

Friends, don't let your current situation discourage you. Brighter days are ahead for the believer in Jesus Christ that refuses to throw in the towel and quit. You've been holding on for so long; hold on for a little while longer. If the test has one hundred questions, why quit at question ninety-seven? The test of life may have been difficult for you up to this point, but there's good news >>> you've made it past the difficulty. You've persevered through challenges, you've battled opposition, you've overcome difficult problems, and you're still standing. Still standing! Every weapon formed against you could not prosper. Every demonic force, every evil altar, every curse, every scheme, every tactic, and every plot of the enemy has failed. You're still standing! For every insufficient resource that you had, God supplied you with His sufficient grace to lead you through the storm. Through Christ you've overcome all things, and you are now more than a conqueror.

The remaining portion of the test of life may be filled with more dilemmas [problems, difficulties], but if we continue to believe and trust in God throughout it all, we'll continue to overcome it all. Psalm 121:7-8 says, "The LORD keeps you from all harm and watches over your life. The LORD keeps watch over you as you come and go, both now and forever" [NLT]. Therefore, let's keep believing, keep hoping, keep trusting, and watch God deliver. Every problem has a solution, but some solutions cause more problems. The best solution for us is God's solution. When your back is against the wall, continue to trust in God.

DEFINE THE PROBLEM | DEVELOP THE SOLUTION

Think about the times when it seemed as if there was no way out and your back was against the wall. God stepped in and made a way out of no way, and gave you the ability to overcome, so remember that every time you face similar challenges. Here's a quick prayer for you, "Father, please help me to have unwavering faith in You and let me not give in to distractions. I commit to believing and trusting in You wholeheartedly. Fill me with the level of faith that I need to always be united with You in spirit and in truth. In Jesus' Name I pray. Amen."

ENCOURAGEMENT OF THE WEEK [#help]

Help is something that we all need in life, but it's also something that we cannot give to everyone or receive from everyone because of limited capacity. God's capacity is unlimited, and His help will always be sufficient for us.

SPREAD THE MOTIVATION [#motivate]

Encourage someone to resist the urge to give up when challenges arise. God always has a solution that is the right solution for us.

Week 49 Motivation
RIGHT IS RIGHT, SIN IS SIN

∞ ∞ ∞

1 John 3:7-10 [GNT]

Let no one deceive you, my children! Whoever does what is right is righteous, just as Christ is righteous. Whoever continues to sin belongs to the Devil, because the Devil has sinned from the very beginning. The Son of God appeared for this very reason, to destroy what the Devil had done. Those who are children of God do not continue to sin, for God's very nature is in them; and because God is their Father, they cannot continue to sin. Here is the clear difference between God's children and the Devil's children: those who do not do what is right or do not love others are not God's children.

Dear Friends,

    If someone asked you to explain the difference between doing what's right and doing what's wrong, what would your response be? If your answer is "I don't know what I would say", I'm asking you now, so, what's your response? This is a question that will likely receive many different responses. Why? Because we tend to allow our feelings and emotions to lead us into deciding what's right and what's wrong. Notice that our feelings and emotions were mentioned, but God wasn't mentioned at all. Shouldn't He have a say in the matter? Of course He should! If not, that would be like a group of toddler children looking after themselves, which may result in a lot of mess, excess sugar, and avoidance of showers/baths. Not good, right? The point is, we can't allow our emotions to help us decide what's right and what's wrong; we must adopt God's standards. Let's look at the featured scripture, which points us in the right direction. It notifies us that doing what's right aligns with righteousness. Doing what's wrong is equivalent to sin, and those that continue to sin belong to the devil because the devil has sinned from the very beginning, which means he is the father of all sin. Let's break that down further.

    All sin is wrong. If you want to see how wrong it is, look at some synonyms of sin, which will include evil, wickedness, immorality, offense, debauchery, and a few other unpleasant terms. That's what sin is; completely unpleasant. No one should ever crave sin, nor should anyone ever be comfortable living with, for, or in sin. Sin is a life destroyer. It will destroy health, relationships, quality of life, and most importantly a true relationship with God. Why? Because the scripture says sin is of the devil, so anyone that continues to sin cannot live for God and still be of the devil. Pop quiz question, what is sin? 1 John 5:17 says, "all wrongdoing is sin" (GNT). Sin is everything wrong; anything that Goes against

God's standards, Word, and will. Some may say that definition isn't helpful for fully understanding what sin truly is, but the scripture helps us with that also, as it indicates that the answer will always be found in Jesus Christ.

*"**There's no need to ponder what's right and what's wrong because Jesus clarifies it all for us, and gives us the Holy Spirit to confirm everything**".*
[#motivated]

Friends, there's no need for any of us to guess what's right and what's sin. If we tried, we'd be lost. Jesus Christ does all of that for us. Jesus is the example of righteousness or what's right. The devil is an example of sin or what's wrong. Jesus came to destroy what the devil had done. If you don't know what the devil did, he deceived the world into accepting sin through disobedience to God. He tricked Adam into exchanging his power and authority for sin. Jesus also enables everyone to become and remain true children of God by giving them God's very nature and filling them with love. Yes, that big "L" word. Love. Doing what's right begins with Jesus Christ. There's a choice to be made, it's either Jesus or the devil. Why? This was discussed in the Bible as Jesus said, "Anyone who is not for Me, is really against Me" (Matthew 12:30, GNT).

There's no need to ponder what's right and what's wrong because Jesus clarifies it all for us, and gives us the Holy Spirit to confirm everything. Universally, we all know that dishonesty is wrong. We all know that abuse is wrong. We all know that greed is wrong. There's no justification for any of it, right? The same can be said for the other sins or wrongdoing. Let's focus on the keyword "continue", as the scripture says, children of God do not continue to sin. That's very important because the word "continue" indicates a repeated decision, which is an intentional choice. Because we are imperfect human beings, flawed since birth, we will make occasional mistakes. I was being kind and generous by saying "occasional mistakes". If I'm being completely honest, the truth is we will mess up many times as we try to figure out life. However, there's a difference between making a mistake and truly repenting for it, which is asking for God's forgiveness and turning away from the wrong behavior, and continuing to intentionally sin and not truly repenting for it. Continuing to do wrong, no matter the justification that is crafted, is wrong. I'm not able to tell you anything other than the truth and I know that the truth hurts at times, so here's the truth >>> "Whoever continues to sin belongs to the devil". That truth may hurt, but it should hurt. It should hurt so much that it prompts you to run straight to Jesus Christ for full deliverance if you're struggling with sin. Run! Leave everything behind and run! He's the One that can save, rescue, deliver, and renew us. He destroyed sin, so why live in destruction? Why live in what He tore down completely? If given the choice, would you live in a pit of destruction surrounded by fire or would you live in a beautiful house filled with love? Jesus said, "There are many rooms in my Father's house, and I am going to prepare a place for you. I would not tell you this if it were not so" (John 14:2, GNT). Don't choose destruction, choose Jesus! He already has a place prepared for you. Remember, right is right, sin is sin.

DEFINE THE PROBLEM | DEVELOP THE SOLUTION

If you've been delivered from a former life of sin, think about where you are now in life. Now, think about the things that you used to do, the way that you used to think, and the damage that could've been done if God didn't deliver you from it. You were a fortunate recipient of God's love. Remember that, especially when temptation of different kinds attempts to pull you back down to that road of sin. Here's a quick prayer for you, "Father, help me to remain fully submitted and committed to You. Help me to not give in to fleshly desires or temptation. Help me to resist all evil and follow Your ways. Help me to accept Your deliverance and cherish it as the invaluable gift that it is. I choose to live wholeheartedly for You. In Jesus' Name I pray. Amen."

ENCOURAGEMENT OF THE WEEK [#sinfree]

It's impossible to please God and sin at the same time. Sin is everything wrong and it opposes God. To really and truly live for God, we must be delivered from all sin. This means maintaining a sin-free heart. God's love for us and the love that He has given us gives us the ability to possess a sin-free heart.

SPREAD THE MOTIVATION [#motivate]

Encourage someone to choose God over the self-destruction of sin that's disguised as fun-filled enjoyment of life. Temporary pleasure will never outweigh eternal life with God.

Week 50 Motivation
HE IS WITH US

∞ ∞ ∞

Isaiah 7:14 [NLT]
All right then, the LORD Himself will give you the sign. Look! The virgin will conceive a Child! She will give birth to a Son and will call Him Immanuel (which means 'God is with us').

Dear Friends,

Do you remember the year 2020? How could we ever forget, right? Although that year was much different than previous years, some things remained the same. For instance, there were still different seasons that occurred, time continued to progress, and even if some people chose not to celebrate Christmas, Christmas day still occurred on December 25th, which means the Christmas messages about the birth of Jesus were still told and shared all over the world. This may seem shocking, but did you know that many people are not fully aware of the story of Jesus Christ? (Hence the reason that you and I are called to spread the Good News about the Lord and Savior Jesus Christ). For those of us that are aware of the story of Jesus Christ, it seems like each year we learn something else about the story that we may have missed before (as is the case with a lot of things in life).

Shifting to the actual message, the featured scripture was a prophecy given to Isaiah to be communicated to King Ahaz who was the king of Judah at the time. In those days, the country of Israel was split into two kingdoms – northern Israel (known as the kingdom of Israel) and southern Israel (known as the kingdom of Judah). If you're wondering why the country was split into two tension-filled kingdoms, check out 1 Kings 12. The featured scripture is preceded by an earlier prophecy that the prophet Isaiah gave to King Ahaz to provide him a sense of comfort after the king found out that the kingdom of Israel was teaming up with Syria to attack Jerusalem (kingdom of Judah). The king and his people were very afraid, so God sent the message to the king (via Isaiah) with the purpose of helping him convert his fear into faith. Following that message, Isaiah delivered yet another message from God, as he said, "Ask the LORD your God for a sign of confirmation, Ahaz. Make it as difficult as you want—as high as heaven or as deep as the place of the dead." But the king refused. "No," he said, "I will not test the LORD like that" (Isaiah 7:11-12, NLT). And that's when God told the king (via Isaiah) that He would give the sign.

That sign would become Jesus Christ. The birth of a Savior. The sign was purposed to remind all of us that God is with us. There's more to the prophecy that followed, which may not be as favorable [positive, encouraging] as one would think, but for the purposes of this message we'll focus on the most important part, and that is the significant sign that would occur.

> *"DON'T FOCUS YOUR ATTENTION ON THE NEGATIVE OR THE UNCERTAINTY. CHOOSE TO FOCUS YOUR ATTENTION ON HIS PROMISE AND GUARANTEE, AND KNOW THAT NO MATTER WHAT'S HAPPENING, GOD IS WITH YOU."*
> *[#motivated]*

Friends, if we were to insert ourselves into the story in those days, would any of us have known what the prophecy meant? "The virgin will conceive a child, she will give birth to a son, and will call Him Immanuel". If I'm being completely honest, I don't think I would've seen the significance, but God! (Fun fact: I've shared this with you already, but this is worth repeating >>> whenever you see or hear "but God!", something is about to follow that makes you want to shout for joy). God knew exactly what would happen, at the right time, and in the right place. If we remember the message provided to King Ahaz, we're reminded that the focus was to convert fear into faith. The message about the birth of Christ was part of that message of faith. If we connect the dots, 'God is with us' is a daily reminder for each of us. The message of the birth of Christ isn't just a story of a one-time occurrence that happened many years ago, it's a promise for a lifetime. It's an everlasting promise and guarantee, especially for today (as it was in 2020). 2020 was unlike most years, months, weeks, and days that we've experienced in the past, as we were constantly surrounded by pandemic uncertainty and fear. Did you know that the residue of fear still lingers today? Instead of being fearful of enemies plotting against us like King Ahaz was, many people are fearful of the unknown, which is causing the most anxiety, panic, and fear than ever before. But God!

God wants us to convert that fear into faith and be reminded of the promise that He is with us. He is with me, He is with you, He is with our neighbors, He is with us all. We're not alone now, nor will we ever be alone, because the promise still stands. The promise is a guarantee, even during times of adversity and turmoil [chaos, disorder]. Therefore, don't focus your attention on the negative (-) or the uncertainty. Choose to focus your attention on His promise and guarantee, and know that no matter what's happening, God is with you. You have a Savior that was born into the world to love you, save you, cover you, protect you, and give you peace with full assurance of knowing that God is with you. This will not change, no matter what happens around us. So, this Christmas and every day that follows, as we reflect on everything that has occurred in our lives, let's always remember that He is with us.

DEFINE THE PROBLEM | DEVELOP THE SOLUTION

If you were living in the year 2020, think about the emotions that you felt. Trusting God to deliver us from those times was the only choice for many of us. What happened afterwards? He reminded us that He is with us always. Therefore, we can trust Him to always be with us, no matter the situation, no matter the circumstance. Here's a quick prayer for you, "Father, please help me to remember that You are always with me. My decision to accept Jesus Christ as my only Lord and Savior has allowed me to be Yours forever. Your covering, protection, guidance, direction, and peace will always be with me. Thank You for being You and doing what You do! In Jesus' Name I pray. Amen."

ENCOURAGEMENT OF THE WEEK [#comfort]

God gives us comfort in knowing that He is with us for an entire lifetime because of Jesus Christ. So, whether things are going good in your life or not so good, know that God is with you because of your decision to allow Jesus to enter your life as your only Lord and Savior.

SPREAD THE MOTIVATION [#motivate]

Encourage someone to know that their faith in Jesus Christ will be rewarded, as God will always be with them for an entire lifetime.

Week 51 Motivation

WHAT WILL YOU DO WITH YOUR TIME?

∞ ∞ ∞

1 Peter 4:7 [NIV]
The end of all things is near. Therefore, be alert and of sober mind so that you may pray.

Dear Friends,

Have you ever considered the importance and overall value of time? If so, do you understand why it's important and valuable? This may be hard to believe, but many people often neglect or undervalue time, which is evident in decision-making. Have you ever planned to do something that was beneficial, but when it was time to do it, you decided to delay doing it? It may have sounded like a good idea when you were planning, but finding motivation to get it done proved to be challenging (need examples? How about exercising, maintaining the budget, reading the Bible every day, etc.). This is highly common due to an unhealthy relationship with time (think about the term "time management"). Yes, it's possible to have an unhealthy relationship with time, just like I had an unhealthy relationship with sugar, specifically with fresh-baked chocolate-chip and oatmeal cookies previously [*insert laughter here*]. It's important for each of us to know that we've been given a very special gift in the form of time. We are allowed to use this gift in the manner that we choose, but keep in mind that although we may be able to do anything, not everything is beneficial for us (1 Corinthians 10:23). It's also important to note that the gift of time has an expiration date that none of us are aware of. In other words, the gift of time is not unlimited or never-ending; it will end at some unknown point. In the featured scripture, we're notified that the end of all things is near, which means time will soon expire for everyone. How soon? Only God knows the answer. This may sound surprising, but it's by God's design that time will expire (read Revelation 21). If this is true for each of us, what will you do with your time while you still have it?

"WE WERE CREATED TO NEED AND DEPEND ON GOD EVERY SECOND OF EVERY MINUTE OF EVERY DAY."
[*#motivated*]

Friends, our most prized possession is the gift of time. It's more valuable than money, it cannot be left behind, and it will finish or come to an end at some point. Unlike money, time cannot be returned or regained if lost or wasted, which makes it extremely important and valuable. Unfortunately, many of us refuse to cherish the gift of time. We choose to waste time or mismanage it by making bad decisions and excluding God from our lives. This should not be. No, this should never be. God gave us the gift of time to use wisely, not to misuse. There's no bigger misuse than to choose to live without God. There's no better choice than to give God our time via our fellowship with Jesus Christ. Have you ever enjoyed spending time with a loved one? Our Father (God) and Savior (Jesus) feel the same way about us. God wants to spend as much time with us as we'll allow Him to. Let's pause right there and think about that for a moment. God, the Almighty Creator, wants to spend time with us, but we must allow Him to spend time with us by extending an invitation to Him. It's almost the same as saying we must give God permission to hang out with us. As farfetched [unbelievable, mind-boggling] and strange as that may sound, it's the truth. He gave us the gift of choice. We choose to open the door of our heart to God and our Savior Jesus Christ. Let's connect this point with our message of time.

Unhealthy relationships with time occur when we choose to give our time to everyone and everything except God. Would you like to conduct a free self-assessment of your relationship with time to determine if it's healthy or unhealthy? Start by determining how much time you spend with God daily and subtract from it the amount of time that you spend interacting with other people or other sources of entertainment. A resulting negative (-) amount should serve as an indicator that something is wrong and your relationship with time is unhealthy and needs improvement. God should never (never, ever) be forced to take a backseat to everything/everyone else in our lives, which will generally result in some form of idolatry. Let's not allow our interaction with God to be limited to a small portion of the day or week, instead let's choose to fellowship with Him throughout the day (each day). If you're wondering, yes, it's very possible to include God in our daily activities. When cooking, invite God into the kitchen with you. When cleaning, invite God to assist you. When studying, invite God to share the best practices with you. When playing games or sports, invite God to join you. When trying to solve problems, invite God to help you. Nothing about us should be off-limits to God. We were created to need and depend on God every second of every minute of every day. Our friends and family are capable of disappointing us, but God will never disappoint us. He'll never leave us nor forsake us if we give Him our time to prove it. Even more, His perfect love is always sufficient for each of us. Our gift of time is decreasing each day, so why not make the best decision now and choose to live wholeheartedly for God through our Savior Jesus Christ? What will you do with your time?

DEFINE THE PROBLEM | DEVELOP THE SOLUTION

Think about your current daily activities and the things that occupy the most time. Those things are the things that are reducing your fellowship time with God. Don't wait until something unfortunate happens in your life for you to choose to spend time with God. Make Him the priority of your life. Here's a quick prayer for you, "Father, please help me to manage my time better by prioritizing You and inviting You to join me in all of my daily activities. Allow me to be fully submitted, surrendered, and aligned to You, always. I commit to giving You all that I have. My heart is Yours. Allow me to never experience life without You. In Jesus' Name I pray. Amen."

ENCOURAGEMENT OF THE WEEK [#goals]

We all have goals, some bigger than others. Motivation and determination may help us achieve goals, but God will always be the deciding Source. When we remain connected to God and stay plugged into Him, the mission, purpose, destiny, and victory becomes much clearer.

SPREAD THE MOTIVATION [#motivate]

Encourage someone to never leave home without God. He's our Compass, Guide, Direction, and Protection for everything we need in life.

Week 52 Motivation

WHAT HAPPENS NEXT?

∞ ∞ ∞

Genesis 6:3 [AMP]

Then the LORD said, "My Spirit shall not strive and remain with man forever, because he is indeed flesh [sinful, corrupt — given over to sensual appetites]; nevertheless, his days shall yet be a hundred and twenty years."

Dear Friends,

Have you ever wondered why humans must die? Have you ever thought about what happens after death on earth? These are both very important questions that are usually thought about when we're younger or as we grow older in life. We'll address both questions in this message. When God created humans, He created us to be His wonderful and perfect creation, free from sin and clothed in childlike innocence. So, what happened? What went wrong? Do you remember the event that took place long ago in the Garden of Eden involving disobedience, a serpent, and forbidden fruit? (Hint, Hint: this is the Adam & Eve story). In those days, God created two very important trees that stood in the middle of the garden, which were the "tree that gives life" and the "tree that gives knowledge of what is good and what is bad". Adam and Eve were allowed to eat from any tree except the tree that gives knowledge of what is good and what is bad. This means that they were allowed to eat from the other important tree, the tree of life. Why? Because God created them to be filled with childlike innocence and have immortality. God didn't want them to lose that childlike innocence, but disobedience occurred after Eve and Adam ate from the forbidden tree. God couldn't allow what was now tainted by disobedience and sin to have access to the tree that gives life and enables immortality (read Genesis 3). God didn't want sin to be rewarded with the ability to live forever (with Him), so He sent Adam and Eve out of the Garden of Eden and blocked everyone from being able to go near the tree that gives life. This started the expiration clock of human life on earth. Humans were granted the privilege of living hundreds of years on earth at one point in time until wickedness increased so much that the LORD decided to put a cap [maximum time allowed] on human life on earth at a hundred and twenty years, with a few exceptions. (Fun fact: Methuselah was 969 years old when he died, which was before the cap on human life (Genesis 5:25-27)). Now, let's proceed to the next question. What happens after death on earth? This all depends on you and me, individually.

*"**DEATH HAS NO POWER OVER THOSE THAT HAVE AN ACTIVE PERSONAL AND INTIMATE RELATIONSHIP WITH JESUS CHRIST.**"*
[#motivated]

Friends, if today was your last day alive on earth, do you know where your next destination would be? Before you answer that, I'm aware of the different beliefs. One belief is that we can't be sure what will happen because only God knows. While that sounds logically acceptable, it's not true. We can be certain of our next destination by the choices that we make while living. Let me explain further and connect the dots. What dots? Keep reading! Remember that tree of life? Remember how no one was allowed to go near it because of sin? Well, it would take a Sinless Savior to lift the restriction and remove the barrier that was placed around it. How would He do it? He would have to somehow, someway take the sins away from human beings, defeat death (because sin results in death), and He would have to give human beings the ability to have a new, born-again life of redemption through Him. Any idea who this Sinless Savior could be? Perhaps, it's the One that said, "Look! I stand at the door and knock. If you hear My voice and open the door, I will come in, and we will share a meal together as friends. Those who are victorious will sit with Me on My throne, just as I was victorious and sat with My Father on His throne" (Revelation 3:20-21, NLT).

That Sinless Savior is Jesus Christ. If we're granted victory over sin, just as Jesus has victory over sin, we will live with Jesus forever. This isn't a maybe, a possibility, or a probably, it's a definitive guarantee. Victory over sin occurs through Jesus Christ. Access to the tree of life occurs through Jesus Christ. It's important for us to remember the childlike innocence that Adam and Eve once had. That's the childlike faith that Jesus requires us to have today. He must be the active focal point of your life. If not, the childlike innocence is vulnerable to deception, just as Adam and Eve were in the garden when they were deceived by the crafty and cunning serpent. The point is that death has no power over those that have an active personal and intimate relationship with Jesus Christ. Jesus Christ is the Way, the Truth, and the Life. No one can get to the Father except through Him (John 14:6). What happens next? It's your decision. Will you choose Jesus Christ and be reconciled to the Father (God)? Or will you choose idolatry and other gods, and be prevented from joining God in His kingdom?

DEFINE THE PROBLEM | DEVELOP THE SOLUTION

Think about a time that your disobedience almost cost you everything that you cherished. That feeling that you felt doesn't compare to eternity without God. It's agony, anguish, and non-stop misery. That's a choice that should never be made. Unfortunately, disobedience to God and obedience to the world will result in that doomed fate. Choose God! Choose Love! Here's a quick prayer for you, "Father, please help me to remain fully obedient to You. Help me to demonstrate the highest level of reverence, faith, and love for You. I cannot live without You, and I never want to attempt to try to live without You. You are my Source for life. I breathe because You give me life. Help me to remain Yours forever. In Jesus' Name I pray. Amen."

ENCOURAGEMENT OF THE WEEK [#choice]

God gave us the gift of choice. We can choose to follow and obey Him or not follow Him by disobeying Him. Both choices have specific consequences. Obedience will result in eternal life with Him. Disobedience will result in eternity away from Him in a place that should be avoided at all costs. What happens next is your choice.

SPREAD THE MOTIVATION [#motivate]

Encourage someone to learn from the mistakes of Eve and Adam and choose to demonstrate their love for God through their continued obedience to Him.

Bonus Week 53 Motivation
FEAR OF MISSING OUT (FOMO)

∞ ∞ ∞

Matthew 7:13-14 [TPT]
Enter through the narrow gate because the wide gate and broad path is the way that leads to destruction—nearly everyone chooses that crowded road! The narrow gate and the difficult way leads to eternal life—so few even find it!"

Dear Friends,

Have you ever joined a popular trend because you didn't want to miss out on the experience or potential reward? If we reflect on our lives and the various life experiences that we can recall, we'll most likely notice a few trends that we followed along with. Think about clothing and fashion trends, hairstyles, speech and slang, food and nutrition, music and entertainment, recreational hobbies, social media, investments, purchases, and the list goes on and on. There's something for everyone to identify, if we look closely, even the things that we should've stayed away from, including wearing skinny jeans that didn't stretch or a slim fit suit after skipping many exercise days [*insert laughter here*]. This means that at some point in our lives, whether briefly or for an extended period, we were influenced by other people or the world around us. Unfortunately, sometimes those influences aren't good.

Consider the feature scripture in which Jesus taught the mass crowds during His popular sermon on the mount (mountainside). In this sermon, He essentially notified the people about two potential life choices. The first choice is the unpopular life choice that may be considered by many to be the less attractive, less fun, ultra-safe, boring choice that many people tend to avoid because of its lack of excitement (narrow gate). The other choice is the super popular life choice that looks exciting, enticing, fun, thrilling, and a bit risky with trendy rewards (wide gate). Just like the people that listened to that sermon many years ago, we have a choice to make as well. We can choose the narrow gate with the narrow road that leads to it, or we can choose the wide gate with the broad road that leads to it. Keep in mind, the gates not only represent different paths in life, but they also represent different destinations. If you need a visualization, think about the narrow gate being the most northern U.S. state that you can think of, and the broad gate being the most southern U.S. state that you can think of (let's go with Maine & Florida). Completely different, right? Which one do you choose?

"RIGHTEOUSNESS IS DRAWN TO GOD AND CAN'T LIVE WITHOUT HIM.
RIGHTEOUSNESS IS NOT INTERESTED IN ACTIVITIES THAT OPPOSE GOD."
[#motivate]

Friends, while the life choice may seem easy, it's important to understand what's behind each choice. It's sort of like the game shows that prompt contestants to select door number one or door number two for the potential prize or surprise. Except in this case, Jesus clearly outlined the result of each life choice, which removed all potential surprises. The "Fear of Missing Out" popular choice will lead to destruction. FYI, FOMO is the acronym for fear of missing out. Is anything more enticing to the world than sin masked as fun? Think about the world (everything that opposes God) and what it offers to those that will accept it. It offers the potential to gain power, get rich and wealthy, have various non-committed intimate and lustful relationships, popularity, influence, and a life of luxury with all of its perks, but all at the expense of you (your soul). All of that stuff is attainable, but it will cost you (your soul), which will cause loss, detrimental strongholds, lack of peace, lost identity, emptiness, curses, emotional trauma, and destruction. Those aren't small fine print items that you'll see on the FOMO road leading up to the wide gate, they're completely hidden from your view. Deception is its weapon of choice and many fall victim to it each day.

On the other hand, the less popular choice is more beautiful than it seems. It's more rewarding, as it will not lead to destruction, but will lead to life, everlasting life with God. This road doesn't have any turns or detours, it's a straight road led by a Guide (Jesus Christ) and a Compass (Holy Spirit). I'm almost certain that you're in the mood to visualize, so picture this Psalm 23:2-3 scripture, "He makes me lie down in green pastures, He leads me beside quiet waters, He refreshes my soul. He guides me along the right paths for His Name's sake" (NIV). Green pastures, quiet waters, refreshed soul, and right paths, all at the hand and direction of God. Not to be misleading, it also mentions walking down a dark valley as well, but being completely protected by God. Does that sound like a bad life choice to you? Your current relationship with God will help you answer that question. Remember, sin is attracted to sin and is turned off by righteousness.

Do you ever feel like you don't have time to pray or read the Bible, but you have significant time to watch TV, browse the Internet/social media, or be entertained by your favorite pastime activities? That's an example of being turned off by righteousness. Righteousness is drawn to God and can't live without Him. Righteousness is not interested in activities that oppose God. Righteousness can discern what's right (God-approved) and what's wrong (disapproved by God). You're the only person that can make life choices for you. It's either God (via Jesus Christ) or it's the world (via Satan). There is no other choice. Which do you choose? Life or destruction?

DEFINE THE PROBLEM | DEVELOP THE SOLUTION

Think about a time that you wanted to follow a popular trend, but you knew that it was the wrong thing to do. What do you think prevented you from doing what you would have regretted? It's no coincidence that you didn't join in on the trend, God protected you. He protected you then and He's protecting you now. Remember His love for you and allow His voice to be the leading voice in your life. Here's a quick prayer for you, "Father, please help me to always choose You, especially when I'm tempted to follow the popular trends and follow my will and not Yours. Help me to not be afraid to be different and always remain faithful to You. Help my life and the choices that I make demonstrate Your perfect love, and may You be glorified, always. In Jesus' Name I pray. Amen."

ENCOURAGEMENT OF THE WEEK [#fomo]

Never be afraid to choose the unpopular narrow gate if that's what God is telling you to do. Prioritize God and what He wants, instead of trying to follow popular trends that will lead you away from God. His will, His purpose, His plan is always the correct choice.

SPREAD THE MOTIVATION [#motivate]

Encourage someone to choose to remain faithful to God, even if it means being different. Different and holy is much better than fitting in with sin.

Bonus Week 54 Motivation
YOU ONLY LIVE ONCE (YOLO)

∞ ∞ ∞

Ephesians 5:15-17 [NLT]
So be careful how you live. Don't live like fools, but like those who are wise. Make the most of every opportunity in these evil days. Don't act thoughtlessly, but understand what the Lord wants you to do.

Dear Friends,

When you hear the phrase "you only live once", what do you immediately think about? FYI, YOLO is used as the acronym. For a lot of people, YOLO is usually a reason to do something out of the norm or outrageously reckless. It's more than choosing to not wear socks with boots or choosing to not have a healthy relationship with lotion in the winter [*insert laughter here*]. YOLO is usually not associated with wisdom. If we take it a step further, it's commonly associated with acts of sin. Why? Because a lot of people are convinced that life can only be enjoyed when sin is involved. Remember, all wrongdoing is sin, and it involves anything that goes against God's standards, Word, and will. Keep in mind, the YOLO-influenced urge to sin isn't new. The Bible references an old YOLO-like saying in 1 Corinthians 15:32 as it says, "as the saying goes, 'Let us eat and drink, for tomorrow we will die'" (GNT). The featured scripture also addresses some of the same issues that we see today. Prior to verse fifteen, we'll notice warnings about sexual immorality, impurity, greed, obscenity, foolish talk, and coarse joking. We'll also notice in verse five that it says that no immoral, impure, or greedy person will inherit the Kingdom of Christ and of God. All of this precedes guidance telling readers to be careful how they live. Is it possible to have fun and truly enjoy life without sinning?

While I can answer that question for myself with a confident "yes", each of us must answer that question for our individual selves. Are you most happy with or without sin? If you don't think that you can enjoy life without sinning, that means you haven't been delivered from your earthly nature (the flesh). Colossians 3 notifies us that sexual immorality, impurity, lust, evil desires, greed, anger, rage, malice, slander, and filthy language are some of the many things that are associated with earthly nature. FYI, the reason that these specific sins were mentioned was because Paul was addressing the matters with a specific audience that dealt with these things at the time, but the message remains applicable to us today, as you can see. If you want to know how God feels about these things, they aren't of Him and don't come from Him, which means He is against them.

"YOU ONLY LIVE ONCE, SO LIVE AS PEOPLE OF LIGHT! THAT'S WHAT THE LORD WANTS US TO DO."
[#motivated]

Friends, you only live once, so why not live the right way? Why not live completely for God? Why not enjoy life and all of its fullness with God and not with sin? There's a misconception that living for God isn't fun. That's completely false and those that choose to adopt that mindset reveal what's in their heart, which is a knowingly or unknowingly craving for sin. Do you crave doing the wrong thing? Do you crave getting drunk or intoxicated? Do you crave falling in lust and having lustful relationships? Do you crave greed and living with no boundaries? If so, that's an indicator that God isn't the priority in your life, which means He may not be in your life because of your choice to accept idolatry. No one should want to live without God. Why? Because we weren't created to do so. The result may not be as pleasant as one may think. Here's the fate for those that choose to live without God:

"Then I saw a great white throne and the one who sits on it. Earth and heaven fled from His presence and were seen no more. And I saw the dead, great and small alike, standing before the throne. Books were opened, and then another book was opened, the book of the living. The dead were judged according to what they had done, as recorded in the books. Then the sea gave up its dead. Death and the world of the dead also gave up the dead they held. And all were judged according to what they had done. Then death and the world of the dead were thrown into the lake of fire. (This lake of fire is the second death.) Those who did not have their name written in the book of the living were thrown into the lake of fire" (Revelation 20:11-15, GNT).

Who are those that did not have their names written in the book? They are those that chose to embrace sin. Those that chose to adopt the YOLO-influenced urge to sin. Don't allow yourselves to be influenced by foolish practices of the earthly nature where the influencers are the "cowards and unbelieving and abominable [who are devoid of character and personal integrity and practice or tolerate immorality], and murderers, and sorcerers [with intoxicating drugs], and idolaters and occultists [who practice and teach false religions], and all the liars [who knowingly deceive and twist truth]" (Revelation 21:8, AMP). Instead, "Let no one deceive you with empty arguments [that encourage you to sin], for because of these things the wrath of God comes upon the sons of disobedience [those who habitually sin]. So do not participate or even associate with them [in the rebelliousness of sin]. For once you were darkness, but now you are light in the Lord; walk as children of Light [live as those who are native-born to the Light] (for the fruit [the effect, the result] of the Light consists in all goodness and righteousness and truth)" (Ephesians 5:6-9, AMP). You only live once, so live as people of light. That's what the LORD wants us to do. What will you do?

DEFINE THE PROBLEM | DEVELOP THE SOLUTION

Think about a time that you wanted to rebel and participate in sinful activities. Did you go through with it? If so, think about the results and think about how much worse things could've been for you and those around you. God's grace and mercy can be abused, which is why we may choose to adopt the YOLO-influenced urged to sin, as we may have been bailed out previously and refused to learn the lessons that should've been learned. Don't make that mistake. Don't allow sin to lead you to self-destruction. God's love for you should be cherished through your obedience to Him. Here's a quick prayer for you, "Father, please help me to avoid sin at all costs. Even when I'm tempted to sin, help me to choose You and Your will for my life. Even when I'm surrounded by sin, help me to remain faithful to You. I want to ensure that my heart, my actions, and my life bring You glory. In Jesus' Name I pray. Amen."

ENCOURAGEMENT OF THE WEEK [#yolo]

You only live once, so will you use that as a reason to ensure that you make the most of your life by making an impact for God? Or will you use that as an excuse to engage in sin-filled revelry and debauchery? It's a decision that each of us must make as we choose to live our lives because You Only Live Once.

SPREAD THE MOTIVATION [#motivate]

Encourage someone to recognize sin for what it truly is, destruction. Sin destroys the relationship with God, which destroys the soul, which destroys any chance of eternal life with God.

Conclusion

AN IMPORTANT DECISION

∞ ∞ ∞

Romans 10:8-13 [NKJV]

"But what does it say? 'The Word is near you, in your mouth and in your heart' (that is, the word of faith which we preach): that if you confess with your mouth the Lord Jesus and believe in your heart that God has raised Him from the dead, you will be saved. For with the heart, one believes unto righteousness, and with the mouth confession is made unto salvation. For the Scripture says, 'Whoever believes on Him will not be put to shame.' For there is no distinction between Jew and Greek, for the same Lord over all is rich to all who call upon Him. For 'whoever calls on the Name of the LORD shall be saved.'"

Dear Friends,

If you're living life alone, if you're lost and seeking answers, if you're wounded and discouraged, then know that God has not forgotten about you. He loves you and has extended His hand of grace and mercy to you. He wants you with Him. He wants you to be a part of His family, His kingdom, and in His presence for eternity. What do you want?

If you're ready to live the purposeful life that God has planned for you, then understand that it all begins with the Lord and Savior Jesus Christ. Life on earth isn't easy. There are challenges, conflict, spiritual warfare, trying times, bad decisions, and much more, but God! God has given each of us direct access to Him through His Son, the Savior Jesus Christ.

So, if you feel led to make the most important decision of your life and are ready to accept (or return to) the Lord and Savior Jesus Christ, do the following with a believing heart:

- **Repent for your Sins**. "Jesus, please forgive me for my sins and help me turn away from all disobedience, idolatry, pride, rebellion, evil, and sin. Create in me a new heart, a clean heart, a humble heart filled with Your love and peace."
- **Confess and Declare your Faith**. "Jesus, I believe that You willingly died on the cross for my sins and was raised from the dead after three days, defeating death, sin, evil and everything that sets itself against the Father (God). Your victory established a place for me in Your kingdom. I receive Your love. I receive Your grace. I surrender my all to You. I humbly submit to You, my Savior. I give You my burdens, my fears, my worries, my pain, and all that I have."

- **Commit to Jesus**. "Jesus, I commit my complete life to You. I cannot live another day without You. Please lead me, guide me, teach me, and direct me throughout this new journey of life with You. Help me in my unbelief, help me to be delivered from evil, help me to discern the traps of evil, and help me to resist temptation to sin. Break all chains and all covenants and agreements with evil. Wash me clean and I will be clean. Save me and I will be saved. Heal me and I will be healed. Deliver me and I will be delivered. You are my Lord and Savior, and I am Yours forever. Amen."

Committing to the Lord and Savior Jesus Christ is the greatest decision that we could make. Now, it's time to remain committed. This requires continued obedience to the Word of God, which will help you abstain from the things that are designed to separate you from God. Disobedience, idolatry, rebellion, and pride are the leading stumbling blocks, so, be on guard. Be covered by God through Jesus Christ. Be submitted and surrendered to Him. Don't add to or take away from His Word. Believe Him, accept Him, and live for Him. He'll be with you when others abandon you. He'll be with you when opposition surrounds you. He'll be with you always. So, live for God through Jesus Christ, forever.

About the Author
MEL FRAZIER-CARROLL

∞ ∞ ∞

Who is Mel Frazier-Carroll? "While I could give you an entire autobiography or an autobiography masked as a biography, I'm going to simply tell you who I am. I am a humble and devoted follower of my only Lord and Savior Jesus Christ. I love God and Jesus Christ with my entire heart, mind, soul, and everything that I have. I was privileged to be invited into the kingdom of God in October 2006, and I have been His ever since. I am married to my life partner, my lovely wife Anna, and we have the honor of 'training up' our three girls, Alyssa, Annalise, and Arielle. I laugh often and smile even more. I am truly filled with the irrevocable peace of Christ, and I am enjoying life with Him. I sincerely enjoy helping others establish and maintain a personal, intimate relationship with the Savior Jesus Christ."

Why This Book? "All credit, honor, praise, and glory belong to God. He gave me the words to write/type, He gave me the ability to relate to others, He gave me the understanding of His Word, and He gave me the privilege of helping others mature in Jesus Christ while representing Jesus Christ. He allowed me to be filled with a desire to humbly encourage others through His Word. I have accepted that gift and responsibility and am grateful that I have been permitted to share the encouragement and motivation with the people that He has allowed me to share it with."

Favorite Scripture? "I don't have a single favorite scripture, but I can tell you that I am motivated by 1 Corinthians 9:19-23 >>> *'For though I am free from all men, I have made myself a servant to all, that I might win the more; and to the Jews I became as a Jew, that I might win Jews; to those who are under the law, as under the law, that I might win those who are under the law; to those who are without law, as without law (not being without law toward God, but under law toward Christ), that I might win those who are without law; to the weak I became as weak, that I might win the weak. I have become all things to all men, that I might by all means save some. Now this I do for the gospel's sake, that I may be partaker of it with you'* (NKJV)."

www.ingramcontent.com/pod-product-compliance
Lightning Source LLC
Chambersburg PA
CBHW080451170426
43196CB00016B/2758